Ruth B. DeMaat

Festival

Festival

GLADIS LENORE DEPREE

ZONDERVAN PUBLISHING HOUSE • GRAND RAPIDS, MICHIGAN

This is a Judith Markham Book
published by Zondervan Publishing House
1415 Lake Drive, S.E., Grand Rapids, Michigan 49506

Library of Congress Cataloging in Publication Data

DePree, Gladis Lenore
Festival! : an experiment in living.

"Judith Markham books."
1. DePree, Gladis Lenore. 2. DePree, Gordon. 3. Reformed (Reformed
Church)—Hong Kong—Biography. 4. Hong Kong—Religious life and
customs. 5. Hong Kong—Social life and customs. I. Title.
BX9541.D46   1986   266'.56'0922 [B]   85-22511
ISBN 0-310-44110-2

Designed and edited by Judith E. Markham

Printed in the United States of America

86 87 88 89 90 91 / 10 9 8 7 6 5 4 3 2

To Nancy
who shared a hot-fudge sundae in Grand Central Station on a magical
day long ago and has kept the faith ever since

contents

the wind in the banyan tree   9

crabshells on the doorstep   19

the devil festival   43

jumping fish   57

light a red candle   75

dance of the dragon   95

a sip of snake wine   117

the other side of the mountain   139

transplanting the papaya tree   157

the festival   175

the wind
in the banyan tree

On the borders of consciousness, a rumbling sound began. First it was like thunder on a distant horizon, then like rain striking the tin roof overhead. Gradually it rose and filled the small white room like the throb of festival drums, pounding, rattling, shaking the senses awake, chasing away the cherished contentment of sleep.

I opened my eyes and looked groggily around the room. The pungent odor of rice-wine swill stung my nostrils, focusing thoughts like a whiff of ammonia.

The swill carts! How could I have forgotten the sound? The rattling, pounding noise was not anything the dream had framed it to be. It was nothing so dramatic as a rainstorm or drums, only the noisy beginning of a day of survival in the fishing village of Chek Wan on Hong Kong Island. It was barely dawn, and the procession from the tangle of huts on the hillside to the wine factory had begun, the crude metal wheels of the old carts striking the rough pavement and jarring the empty swill pails with a deafening clatter.

Above the din, the deep, earthy voices of women rose rich and mellow in the foggy dawn, high and low like calling-songs.

"Jo-sun, have you drunk early tea yet?"

"May-a, not yet!"

"Deem guy-a? Why not?"

"Ah yah, one must make a living first!"

"Hah! Must the pigs drink before you do?"

"Haih-a! They bring more in the market!"

Laughter . . . the absurd juxtaposition of a pig's worth and a person's cup of tea . . . rich, melodic laughter . . . the clatter of carts . . . and the pounding of the surf on the beach just below the narrow street.

I lay fully awake, jarred by the sounds in the street below. The fishermen's calls echoed back and forth, signaling the end of the night's work. The nets were being hauled in with great wet splashes, and the crackle of fires lighted for breakfast mixed with the pounding surf. Dogs yelped, and hungry pigs squealed on the distant hillside. I suddenly felt as though life were going on without me while I lay in this quiet, white room.

A stab of guilt-curiosity propelled me to my feet.

I glanced at Gordon, sound asleep, and decided not to wake him. He was still tired from shepherding four children, twenty-one pieces of luggage, two baseball bats, an image of the Goddess of Mercy, and a wife who felt he was stopping in too many countries at hotels with shower knobs that fell off, over the ten thousand quite odd miles between New York and Hong Kong. I looked at him and smiled: the inexhaustible was exhausted. But what did it matter now? We were *home*.

Moving quietly out through the storm-warped doors and onto the tiled third floor balcony, I stood overlooking the street.

It caught at me as soon as I stepped into it again: the same instantaneous, visceral reaction I had remembered when describing this village to anyone who would listen . . . a purely primal fascination, a deep pull that left one spellbound beyond all reason, the feeling that some basic life process was taking place here, raw and unadorned, if one could but see it.

This was the way I had remembered it in the year away—each tree and rugged stone wall, each curve of the sea and turn of the narrow street—and now I looked at it cautiously, hungrily, as one looks at the face of a long-lost friend, afraid it might have changed, might have become estranged in some elusive way.

Scene by scene I checked it against my memory. The stretch of sea, reaching to the right until it touched the morning sky . . . the fishing junks with their white or rust sails catching the first rays of morning sun . . . the sandy beach marked with white foam at the water's edge . . . it was the same. The winding street that ran beneath the balcony, past the weather-beaten cypress tree, and through the dark tunnel-like buildings of the wine factory was the same. And the other street that turned sharply at the corner where our rain-streaked stucco house stood still ran past the rough stones and red roof of the factory's west side. I knew the ancient banyan tree still stood around the corner because it had stood there forever with the smoldering sandalwood sticks under it; and by the many calls from the sellers of fruits and vegetables, I knew that the market stalls, so silent when we passed them late last night, were opening for the day as they did every day.

It was all the same, yet something had changed.

The sea pounded and boomed on the beach, and I stood on the balcony, drinking in the wind and open to all the scenes below me. Perhaps *that* was the difference. Two years before when we had come to the village to live for the first time, it had been Gordon's idea. Between the village and me there was always the buffer of Gordon. If it rained seventeen days in succession and the towels had to dry on the stairway, it was Gordon's idea. If the children ate salted dried squid and developed stomach upsets, it was Gordon's idea. If something extremely beautiful happened, it had all been Gordon's idea, and I admitted *he* had been right in moving here.

But now there had been the year away: a year spent in America thinking about the village and dreaming of coming back. In those months I had discovered that distance lent enchantment to typhoons, lizards, moldy shoes, and a perpetual feeling of loneliness. And somehow, by talking about the village to anyone who would listen and scribbling down ideas in the middle of the night, I had unwittingly fallen in love with this spot of earth. For me, the village had become a reason for being, a place where I could explore life.

Yes, the village was the same. It was I who had changed.

The narrow street between the house and the sea was filled with early morning risers now, and I peered down, hoping to see a familiar face. Perhaps Tommy Jau or Wing or the Jeng boys. For a moment I thought I spotted Pearl from the rice shop, but all I could see were the tops of heads with feet moving under them like wind-up toys. Even the wine-swill carts were flattened out until only the rusty tops of buckets showed, edging the yellow circles of steamy wine swill. From the balcony, the street was an abstract drama of faceless beings, with the swish-pound-boom of the sea. I watched until the movement of colors seemed dreamlike, something half-remembered, something I should know, or once knew.

I leaned over the railing, drawn into the scene. Out across the water, where the boatmen were spreading their nets to dry, they seemed to be asking me some question, beckoning for some response . . . as though I must in some way capture them. For a moment I wanted to get a camera, and then I thought of photos lying in a drawer and knew that was not what was expected of me.

The sea breeze caught in the ancient branches of the banyan tree, and they tossed and signaled sagely and slowed to a whisper. I strained to hear, but there were no words . . . *and I stood between the sea and the wind and the ancient stones of the street, almost in touch with some vital force that lay beneath the visible or audible expressions of life.*

I shook my head and breathed in the salt air in great hungry gulps and shivered. What was the strange, primitive power of this place?

The procession of carts pounded back and forth over the pavement and disappeared into the dark passage of the factory street. The building itself had a certain mystique. It was said to be haunted by the owner's former wife, who had hanged herself when he took her servant as a mistress. But this morning the wine factory was the center of business. Smoke boiled out of its chimney, mixing with the morning fog. The aroma of fresh rice-mash wafted over the village like the smell of a huge vat of breakfast cereal, and the swill collected during the night fed the endless line of carts.

By the entrance to the dark tunnel, an old woman in a black pajama and faded blue apron set up shop on two orange crates crossed by a rough board. A large basin of dark red bean soup, a few blue bowls and spoons, a bucket of water and a rag, and her breakfast counter was ready to serve the line of women waiting at the smoky grey factory door. Small children, wedged in among the pails on the carts, opened their mouths birdlike to be fed. The old woman scooped up beans, pocketed the coins, dipped the dishes in the pail, gave them a wipe, and was ready for her next customer.

On the other side of the tunnel a small boy had set up a pickle stand. Directly behind him was a new red sign. It said NO ENTRY. For a moment the relationship between the sweet bean soup and pickles for breakfast and the NO ENTRY sign gave a twist in my stomach. As much as I loved this village, would I ever fully *enter* into it? Could I ever eat bean soup and pickles for breakfast? Would I ever know enough legends to understand the jokes? Would even Gordon's daily exposure to a thousand students or my life on this street day after day ever get us beyond the NO ENTRY sign that seemed to guard the secrets of the East?

I decided not to look at the sign and not to believe it.

The faceless crowd below passed and came and passed again in kaleidoscopic patterns. An old European who lived up on the hillside among the huts passed, coming home from his morning dip at the far beach. His head looked curiously soft and pink among the thickly covered dark heads in the street.

I followed the pink head through the crowd and wondered why he lived on the hillside among the huts. There were rumors that he had turned traitor during the Japanese occupation of Hong Kong and had been banned from the European community. The small boys of the village hooted after him and called him "The Fox." Why did he live here?

Of course, others might wonder the same about us. Why did we, an American man and woman with four young children, choose to live in a Chinese village? Were there strange rumors about us as well?

The reasons, if they were reasons, had seemed clear enough two years ago when we had moved to Chek Wan to spend a few euphoric months on this street before going back to New York for a year's study. It was the end of the sixties, and the fresh breeze of change had reached hurricane proportions. Tradition was being thrown to the winds, and the only relevant answer to any question was "Why not?"

And Gordon and I, involved with students in an Anglo-Chinese educational project, had gradually over a ten-year period asked ourselves deeper and deeper questions, until one day we decided to leave the American circle in which we lived and move to Chek Wan village.

Why?

Our Chinese neighbors in the village had asked us frankly if we had come to change them or because we felt sorry for them as some Americans did. We said, "No, a thousand times no. We have come to learn, to share your rich way of life, to understand your customs, to celebrate your festivals, and experience your way of thinking . . . to live your lives with you. Perhaps you will change us."

The villagers had shaken their heads and smiled, saying they had never heard of such a thing.

When our European or American friends asked us, we gave a different answer: one that dealt with our concern over barriers between people, with the need for unconditional respect between persons, with the need to discover and overcome our own unconscious prejudices, and with the desire to participate in a lifestyle that sprang from different historical and theological roots than our own. We spoke about submerging ourselves in a reality so deeply different that we could perhaps become more objective about all forms of reality, including our own. The first ten years in Hong Kong had already taught us to break through our shallower walls of prejudice. But now it was the denser walls, the subtler divisions of culture and tradition, that intrigued us—the attitudes toward myths and legends, the place of festivals and rituals in a people's inner lives.

When we asked ourselves in private conversations, we had both begun to suspect that what we believed about God was too small for the complex world we were discovering. It was not a loss of faith but a wondering if we had come to shallow conclusions about our faith too early in life and with too little thought. An unexplored sense of wonder seemed to call to us, to make us less quick to give accustomed answers to old questions. What lay beneath the forms and rituals of our own culture? What unifying elements lay under the scattered bits of preformed belief we had accepted as children? The search was indescribable—more a wistful listening than an actual question.

Why . . . there were many answers to the question *why,* all of them true, all of them incomplete. But on this morning with the excitement of return new and the keenness not yet blunted, I knew why we were here. It was because of the wind in the banyan tree, whispering secrets we had not yet caught . . . secrets that intrigued.

Gordon was awake and dressed when I went back into the house. I should have caught the difference in his mood, but I was drunk with the sea air, with the sun on the sails, with the sounds of the street.

"I finally have it!" I said, wrapping my arms around his sizable chest and giving him an excited hug.

He looked down at me with kind abstraction in his eyes. "Have what?"

"The feeling that must have brought you here. It practically pulls you out of yourself, doesn't it? And the strange thing is, I don't even love this place because of you any more—I mean, I think I'd love it here even if you didn't. You're not pulling me any more; I'm walking beside you under my own steam. Do you know how few people in this world have a chance—" I paused midsentence, sensing that his thoughts were elsewhere.

"Do you remember it like *this?*" he asked suddenly.

"I think so. In fact, it's even more exciting than I remember it."

His eyes searched the walls, and following them, I noticed the rainstreaks that left a black trail from window sill to floor. The curtains were ringed with yellow watermarks and dotted with grey mildew. A lizard ran across the ceiling devouring mosquitoes.

"When do you think you'll get around to washing the curtains?" he asked quietly.

I felt my world narrow to the white room again, this time not so white.

"That's mildew, Gordon. Mildew doesn't wash out. It's from the sea air."

"My mother used bleach on her curtains, and they were always white. Shall we make the bed?"

I gave the sheet an angry yank. "Gordon, this is not Michigan, and I am not your mother. You can't have everything at once. If you wanted white curtains you should have bought a little white house and trained me to be domestic. But as it is, you have taken me to this village on the other side of the world, where people don't even *have* curtains, and you still want *white clean* curtains. You *do* want the best of both worlds!"

It was quiet except for the bed-making noises. I felt ashamed for being so impatient, but I was still full of the wild sea air and wanted him to share my enthusiasm.

"But whatever we have to give up here, it's worth it, don't you think so?" I asked in a conciliatory tone. "I mean, think of what we've got going here . . . an experiment in a completely new lifestyle . . . a chance to experience living in the third world first hand . . . a chance to bring up four children without racial bigotry . . . even a chance to take a good look at our own sense of integrity. And you're worrying about *mildew?*"

"I know," Gordon said thoughtfully. "I couldn't sleep last night thinking about those very things. And I'm beginning to ask another set of questions . . . or maybe they're the ones you asked when we came here. Can we really become persons who experience third world living firsthand, or is this a game we're playing? I mean, would you like to cancel our check from New York and raise pigs on the hillside?"

"But—"

"And do we know that we are going to raise our children without prejudice and bigotry, or are they going to feel they've been forced to live out our strange ideas, isolated from their countrymen? Will they grow up and rebel against us and hate everything we stand for?"

"I don't—"

"Just a minute. Let me finish. Do you think we can really afford to take a good look at our values? We might have some kind of illusion that we're *avant garde,* but when you face the realities, we represent the establishment in every way: the educational establishment, the religious establishment, the establishment of our government. Can we really question any of these things or our relationship to them and still know who we are . . . even keep our *job?*"

I felt all of the sea air go out of me, along with a good deal of my own. "But Gordon, you're regressing, you're—"

"I'm being responsible, and in the end, I *am* responsible, unless you want to go out and raise pigs."

There was a hint of a smile on his face, but I was not in a mood to be teased. There was too much at stake.

"But we signed a lease. A five-year lease—"

"No, I forgot to tell you . . . I only signed for three, and two of those years are up. The rents are going up all over Hong Kong, and I wouldn't be surprised if the landlord would double what he's asking for this place when the lease comes up for renewal in April."

"But that's only ten months from now. I thought we were going to *stay* here—"

"Ten months is long enough to get the feel of how it's going to work."

"But you can't do this!"

"Why not?"

"When I finally agreed to come here, you said you'd stay here until the kids grew up. We have moved fourteen times, and—"

"But what if it doesn't work out?"

"Then we should *make* it work. The idea is right. We're going in the right direction, and I think we should have the determination to make it work. You've got your work at school, but I need this place. *I'm not ready to leave yet!*" I felt the edge of tears coming in my voice.

"Come on now," he said soothingly, "if it works, we'll stay. No problem. But what I'm saying is that if it doesn't, we should be free to move on. Look at all the people we know who've gotten themselves caught in some 'meaning trap' and are miserable. I think meaning should grow out of your life naturally, not forcibly. I can't live that way."

I buried my face in his shirt, ashamed to be crying on my new independence.

"I can't figure you out," I sighed. "Every time I get where you are, you aren't there anymore. Are you ever going to settle down?"

He raised my face and traced the wet marks with his fingertips. "Probably not," he said solemnly. "But you'll still come along, won't you?"

I looked at his face and remembered the first time I had seen it across a room; my heart had nearly stopped. *I remembered it dark and shaded the night we promised our love to each other. I remembered walking in crunchy leaves and kissing in corners, remembered standing on a sand dune together and looking into a future so full of love it needed no heaven.*

I remembered holding newborn children, fresh with the miracle of birth, helpless, complete, alive, almost frightening in their wonder, the creation we had shared together.

You'll still come along, won't you?

Yes, but not yet . . . not yet!

Outside the window there is a street, and inside of me there is a new and terrible need to discover as large and mysterious as love or birth.

I went to the bathroom to splash water over my face and heard the children waking up downstairs. I glanced in the mirror, and my face looked different. A strange, new feeling sparkled in my eyes—a sensation of love and freedom that sent me soaring yet at the same time held me down in a deep responsibility to time and persons. Any secrets discovered in this search would have to be delved after in the firm context of a family, and if I could not convince Gordon otherwise, in the space of ten months.

I glanced outside and listened to the wind once more, then went downstairs to make breakfast.

crabshells
on the doorstep

A crowd of village children was sitting on our doorstep. I heard them chirruping inches away on the other side of the thick door as I passed on my way to the kitchen.

It was hot and stuffy in the tiny whitewashed room. I turned the rusty key and swung the glass doors out into the open courtyard, letting the fresh sea air in. Our four children were already outside, exploring the roofless enclosure, running in and out of the orange door that led to the street and the banyan tree.

I stood in the middle of the floor, immobilized by two thoughts at once: there was nothing in the house to eat, and the branches of the old tree drooping above the courtyard stirred in me a feeling of complexity. As sage as its whisper might sound from the balcony, here on street level the sagacity of life under its branches might be questioned. One thing must be admitted: it was versatile. Under its branches the village garbage was collected, sandalwood sticks were burned for prayers to the spirits, men listened to the dog races and gambled away their money, the village carpenter built furniture, and up beyond the gambling shed there was even a hut where two addicts lived together, dreaming their opium dreams. Some activities under the banyan tree seemed beautiful; some ugly. Was it possible to absorb one without the other? Or was the secret of this street something beyond either beauty or ugliness?

The heavy wooden door opened, and Gordon came in from the street with a bag of groceries. He was dripping with perspiration and a certain provident smile.

That solved problem number one. Problem number two would take longer.

We sat around the table that morning of our new beginning, eating our usual eggs and toast and feeling a new urgency. Gordon, the tall, dark, big-shouldered man with the calm face, looked hesitant as he listened to the motley street sounds. Michael, the eleven-year-old with blond, thatched-roof hair, seemed uneasy and tapped his foot under the table. Marita, his twin sister with long blond curls and keen blue eyes, looked from one parent to the other, trying to sense what was going on. Deidra, the slim, dark-eyed chatterbox of nine, kept up a constant flow of talk about who she would see and what she would do. And Christopher, the little fellow of two and a half, complacently ate his egg.

I watched him poke egg into his mouth, wondering if some mother hen would be shocked if she knew the egg she had laid intending it to become a chick would become a part of a human child instead. *How strange it was that a chick could become a child, that life forms could be absorbed into each other and change form.*

Gordon's deep morning rumble interrupted my egg thoughts.

"Now kids, I want you to be open and friendly. Take the village people for what they are and try to learn all you can."

Marita's answer was quick, like a wound-up spring released. "Of course we'll take people for what they are," she said. "What's the matter with what they are?"

Gordon hesitated, thrown off guard.

"Could we please go swimming *now?*" Mike asked, tapping his foot faster.

"All right, but be sure the lifeguard is on duty."

"I'm going swimming too," Chris said, climbing out of his highchair.

"No, you can't go now. I'll take you later," I promised.

They were away from the table, in a hurry to get out of the tense hot atmosphere of the house and into the cool seawater. We sat sipping our coffee, watching the small swim-suited figures escape out the doorway.

"Are you sure the beach is lifeguarded this early in the morning?" Gordon asked.

"Don't worry. They're all good swimmers."

It was a familiar conversation, but the speakers had switched lines.

There was a knock on the door. Gordon opened it, and the bird sounds of the children on the doorstep, the rumble of the carts, and the pounding of the sea rushed in.

In the doorway stood Wing Sung and Yau, wonderfully familiar yet somehow changed, perhaps not so much changed as deepened. Everything they had been a year ago, they were more of now. Wing Sung, the cautious friend with the wiry hair and angular face, looked even more cautious and angular. Yau, the eager-faced, bright-eyed optimist, seemed to have a more intense hopefulness shining in his black eyes.

We made places for them at the table, exchanged greetings and family small talk, and offered them tea and toast.

Wing Sung accepted the tea, but Yau smiled his bright smile.

"Please, do you have more coffee?" he asked in his best English. "Your coffee smells so good!"

"Coffee?" I laughed incredulously. "I didn't know any self-respecting Chinese even drank coffee for breakfast. Are you changing into a *Siyan* like us?"

"Mebee," he grinned mischievously. "Since you are gone, I even got a new name. My teacher in the English school gave me the name Tommy. You think I look like a Tommy?"

I could see him with his straight hair brushed over one eye, white collar, bow tie, and short pants: little Tommy Tucker sings for his supper. Something about the desperate eagerness in his eyes did look like a Tommy.

"Why did you need a new name?" Gordon asked.

"Why did you?" Tommy countered. "You came and took the Chinese name of Ding. What was wrong with your American name?"

"I got tired of people calling me everything from DeTree to DoPee."

"Hiah-a! And you should hear how the Siyan say a name like Yau Chung Choi . . . ah yah! I think if the world is getting so mixed together we all need two names, yes? Mebee many names!"

Wing Sung sipped his tea, hesitant amusement in his eyes.

"Some people go around sticking their teeth out," he said pointedly. "One name is good enough for me."

There was a flicker of antagonism in Tommy's eyes, and he answered with a tinge of scorn in his rapid-fire Chinese. "Wing Sung is a *Bou-sau,* one who feels he must protect the old ways. His mother has trained him well. He thinks nothing should ever change. I, personally, am not that pleased with the way things are."

"Haih, I agree with you that conditions of living could be changed, but not all the customs and traditions that you would laugh at and sweep away!"

"Customs and traditions?" said Tommy. "Those are the root of no change! Mindless repetitions that go nowhere. And tell me this . . . what is going to happen to all the traditions we carry on in this village when the next few generations die out? Already in mainland China, these stupid superstitions are forbidden. People in this village are observing customs that no longer exist!"

"No longer exist? How can you say they no longer exist? The festivals of this village will be here as long as this village. Without them there would be no *sin-hau,* no order or pattern to the year, no meaning, no *flavor* . . ."

"But they contain the seeds of stupidity. They're for the old women, for the superstitious and the foolish. Who needs them? I feel meaning and flavor every time the sun rises in the morning!"

"Hah!" retorted Wing Sung. "And what about when it *doesn't?*"

Gordon and I sat quietly, sipping our coffee, knowing that we would again be in the midst of dialogue. It was almost as though the house of the Siyan were a place where things could be said that could not be said on the open street.

We were clearing the breakfast table that morning when Gordon asked me, "Are you going to have household help this time?"

"I don't know," I said slowly. "I want to think about it first."

At every stage of living in the East it had been a question, to have or not to have household help. There had been a time when the children were all smaller that help was almost a necessity, being ten thousand miles away from relatives. But this time it hardly seemed to fit the whole feeling of noncomplexity we were reaching for. Somehow, washing my own family's clothes helped me keep in touch with them . . . *whose socks had holes and whose jeans were out at the knee* . . . there was something impersonal and disassociated about not knowing such facts. And then the whole area of relationships with people in the village had to be considered carefully. Would I be thought standoffish and lazy, careless of money and decadent if I hired someone from the same street to do my work? It had been different when we lived in the western sector and a servant came in . . . but somehow the idea of a household helper who was a neighbor on this street seemed confusing.

I thought of the twenty-one bulging suitcases full of clean and dirty clothes of all seasons sitting upstairs and of the primitive methods we had for washing . . . of the water to be boiled for drinking, and the mold streaks to be scrubbed off the walls.

And then I heard the rumble of the pig carts outside, the swill carts with the children on them rattling back and forth since dawn, and decided that my life was at worst infinitely softer than theirs. I could at least do my own housework.

Gordon was going to the school for the day, and I decided to walk into the market. With Chris on one hip and a woven market basket in the opposite hand, I stepped out the front door. The makeshift stalls on the corner by the wine factory had done a brisk business, and the three steps between our door and the street were covered with small children eating bowls of bean soup and delicacies from the pickle jars. They looked at us in mild surprise, as though they wondered why we were walking on their breakfast table.

"Jo-sun, good morning," I said. "Would you loan us a little bit of room to walk through?"

Two small girls with shiny black hair hitched up their trousers and allowed us to pass.

The familiar smell of rice wine, sea air, and country sanitation hit my senses as I walked under the banyan tree. I glanced up to where its branches reached for the sky and down to where its roots grasped the earth like an old gnarled hand. Fragrant sticks of sandalwood smoldered under the tree, sending grey curls of smoke skyward that temporarily obliterated other odors.

Just beyond the tree sprawled the establishment of Chun's carpenter-shop home. The shop was open-fronted, so it was never any secret what the Chuns were doing. Chun Sang was bent over a sawhorse, planing a piece of wood with long strokes that made his sunburned arms stand out in muscular knots. Gentle faced young Chun Tai moved among the profusion of shavings, baby beds, tables, household gods, television set, and potty chair with the cheerful grace of a gentle bird. On her back was strapped a new infant, so small it hardly made a lump in the *mei-dai,* which held it.

Chun Tai waved and came to the front of the shop, a bundle of sandalwood *heung* in her hand. It was the sixteenth by the lunar calendar, and devout persons all over the village were burning heung.

"Ding Tai." She smiled. "How is your son?"

"Chun Tai, Congratulations! You have a new one!"

She grinned wryly. "What congratulations?" She laughed. "It's only a girl!"

"May I see?" I knew the other two children were sons, and her disdain could not be genuine.

Chun Tai reached behind her and lifted the sun cloth from the tiny face. The child's head was exquisitely molded with dark hair, long lashes, and a tiny pink rosebud mouth.

"Ahh, . . ." I breathed. "How beautiful she is!"

A look of fear crossed Chun Tai's face, and too late I remembered. Until a child was a month old it was dangerous to acknowledge its presence, much less stand in the open street and proclaim its beauty. There were always jealous spirits in the world, trying to destroy beauty, and to boast of one's child was to invite its destruction.

Chris reached out and touched the tiny face with a gentle finger. Chun Tai nervously lit two fragrant heung and stuck them in an earthen pot. I watched the smoke ascend and the relief spread over her face. The carelessness of boasting had been counteracted.

She nodded and smiled.

"Ho," she said. "When you're free, come and sit awhile."

On down the street, past the boat-children's school, a row of stalls stretched long and narrow under a single sun-baked roof. Wong Tai squatted on the pavement in a flowered *sam-fu,* her round cheery face squinted against the smoke of the wood fire she was poking. Red flames rose lazily in the heat and licked the brown ceramic pot of water. She looked young and perky, hardly old enough to be the mother of Wing Sung and five other children, hardly efficient enough to manage the retail fish business while her husband Wong Sang ran the wholesale end.

"Wai, Wong Tai!" I called.

Her face uncrinkled and flashed a smile.

"Ah, Ding Tai, Tisso," she called, using the pet name the village had given Chris. "I saw Ding Sang this morning. Ah yah, Tisso." She pinched both his cheeks. "So white and fat! What do you feed these Siyan babies, Hah? Ah yah, tell me, where do you like it best, in *Mei Gwok,* the Beautiful Country or here? Which people are best, Americans or Chinese?"

"Ah, Wong Tai, what can I say? You know not *all* the good people in the world could possibly be Chinese!"

"Ah yah, Ding Tai." She smiled. "Come and have a cup of tea with me."

We squatted on the pavement together, waiting for the water in the pot to boil while Chris chased a chicken. The sun beat down mercilessly on the concrete, sending up corrugated heat waves and the fetid odor of the fish market.

"Wah!" I said. "How can you drink hot tea when the sun is already like a ball of fire?"

"Ah, tea is cool," she assured me. "Tea cools the body chemistry. If I drank ice water like you Siyan, I'd die of the heat!"

We looked at each other and laughed, content to be friends and to be different. But in the flash of Wong Tai's laughter something was transmitted, the feeling that on this street, one drank tea and accepted all the way of life that went with it. People drank tea; the rest were non-people.

I drank Wong Tai's tea.

Tall, thin Mok Tai was chopping meat for a customer when we passed the Mok family stall. The old grandfather dozed out front, soaking up the sun. Mr. Lew, the cripple, was hopping around his vegetable baskets, nearly bent double with his infirmity. He was the only person on the street who was habitually drunk, and it was excused because his back pained him. Behind the piles of fresh greens, Mr. and Mrs. Lee were tending their popular vegetable stall, the one stall that had monthly accounts for the Siyan who came into the market from other areas to buy vegetables. They were already clustered around the Lee stall this morning. The broad-hipped European wives in cotton dresses and sandals looked gigantic next to tiny Mrs. Lee in her cotton sam-fu.

Across the street and up the stone steps there were other foreigners going into the Store, the only other monthly-account establishment in the village. The Store was almost exclusively patronized by foreigners, and the smell of long-dead frozen meats, strange packets, mixes, wheat flour, and strong drink made its air almost poisonous to the village people. The servants of the Siyan bought there, and young boys who needed bread and sardines for a picnic, or children from the street who wanted popsicles, but the Store, for all intents and purposes, was a Western convenience. Its goods were sold as one might sell drugs not because of any taste for them but because of the profit. And strangest of all, the Store was run by the Hong family, leading Communists in the village.

Rounding the corner, we nearly bumped into fat Mrs. Yau, Tommy's mother. She clapped me on the shoulder, pinched Chris's cheeks, hugged us both, and boomed in her deep, earthy voice, "Ah yah, Ding Tai, what the devil! What are you doing back here! My son Chung Choi, he says he's Tommy now. Tom-my, wouldn't that kill you? Ah yah,, what a name! The name I gave him isn't good enough. Ah yah, that's the way these young ones are now . . . ah yah! It's good as the devil to see you!"

Her motions were squirrel-quick, like Tommy's, in spite of her size. She picked up a handful of vegetables from the pile and pushed them in my basket with an air of secrecy. "Don't tell Mr. Lee," she whispered hoarsely. "He'll kill me. A gift. Remember I didn't sell that to you. I'm not robbing his customers. A gift, to Ding Sang."

She laughed huskily above the noise of the traffic, and I laughed with her, amazed at her ability to smile at all. For some reason Tommy had never explained, his father had left the village a few years ago, and Yau Tai was stranded with six children. She was up early, buying vegetables; up late selling vegetables. Her children slept in a makeshift shelter behind the vegetable crates, one son was badly handicapped, and every Sunday the children had to mind the stall while she went to parts unknown to visit her husband. Yet here she stood this morning laughing, filling my basket with gifts . . . a person so much more than the sum of all her problems. Whatever was the secret of this street, she must have found it.

The Jeng's rice shop rose out of the dimness of the narrow street along the beach. Jeng Tai rushed around among the rows of rice barrels, vats of oil, and bottles of soy sauce, giving instructions to her four teenage sons and her daughter China Pearl. It was the busy time of the morning, Jeng Sang was out delivering, and everyone had come to buy provisions for the eleven o'clock meal.

Jeng Tai looked up and waved, her round cheeks flushed with business. "Ayie, Ding Tai, please come in and sit!"

"Not necessary, Jeng Tai, you're busy. I only want to buy a little rice."

"No, no, no, come in and sit! China Pearl, pour Ding Tai some tea. Ah yah, long time I haven't seen you. Sit here until I can sit with you." She pulled up a wooden stool and patted it.

I came and sat on the stool. China Pearl poured tea from a green thermos with red roses on it and gave it to me. She was a lovely looking girl, seventeen, and the object of much wishful thinking among the village boys. I had heard the boys tease Tommy about her, to which he protested, "Hah, Jeng Tai will see to it that whoever marries that one has more money than I'll ever have!" But China Pearl was beautiful. Her face had that winsome kittenlike piquancy that is a gift of oriental beauty, and her hair fell straight, black, and shiny to her waist. In some ways she looked as though she were too refined for the rough surroundings of the rice shop.

I sat obediently on the stool, sipping tea and looking around while Chris chased a striped ginger cat through the rice sacks. The shop was the Jeng's home as well as place of business. A ladder led from the main floor to a cockloft where the Jeng boys slept. China Pearl's room was a corner next to the rice shop. The parents shared another small enclosure just large enough for a double bed, and the kitchen was a small closetlike room with a strap-hinged door leading out to the beach.

I glanced into the kitchen, expecting to be appalled by its smallness and its inconvenience, but what struck me was something quite different. It was nothing but a concrete slab with a place for a fire, a wok, and a few earthen pots, but it had a smoky beauty, as though everything in the room had grown that way from some organic matter, as if the stones might as easily rearrange themselves before my eyes. I looked at the delicate patterns of the smoke-marked walls and the crude strength of the earthy utensils, thought of the delicious foods Jeng Tai created, and wondered what was the use of all the complex kitchens I had known, had wanted.

When we left the rice shop, Jeng Tai had heaped noodles into the basket, which she insisted were for Christopher (after soundly pinching his cheeks), and instructed China Pearl to go home with us and show me how to cook them.

It was delightful to walk along the shaded beach street with the girl and see it through her eyes. She paused at the snake-wine shop and pointed out the large glass jars of wine with the mottled coils of brown-black snakes looped neatly in serpentine spirals.

"Have you ever tasted snake-wine?" she asked mischievously.

I shivered. If becoming a part of this street meant drinking *that,* it would be hard to pass the test.

"Not yet," I admitted. "Have you?"

"My brothers made me drink some once, for a joke," she said.

We walked, chatting and stopping to see the shops until we came out at the wine factory, just at the point where the NO ENTRY sign guarded the dark tunnel from vehicle traffic. After the morning in the street I wanted to turn around and smile at the sign, to tell it how wrong it was . . . but then I remembered there were always jealous spirits around, wanting to destroy anything beautiful, and I must be careful not to boast in the open street.

The children came home from the beach, hungry and sunburned. China Pearl and I chopped Yau Tai's greens, cooked Jeng Tai's noodles, and set the big table in the dinning room with a stack of bowls and chopsticks. Wing and Tommy came from somewhere, half the children from the front steps found their way in the front door, our own children were somewhere in the crowd, and we all ate noodles.

I skimmed about, feeling an unreal sense of utopia. *Food had come . . . food was going . . . the names and faces were all friends, whether known before or not.* The wind rushed up from the beach, banging the doors and windows like cymbals, and I would not have been at all surprised if music had come rolling up out of the sea at the wave of my chopsticks. *If only Gordon were here now,* I thought, *he would be willing to stay forever. This is how life should be . . . ayie, this is heaven!*

That afternoon I began pulling things out of the kitchen shelves. The glimpse into the Jeng kitchen had driven me a little mad. I pulled out stacks of dishes, extra pots and pans, bowls . . . it was as though I must rid myself of things that were cluttering up my existence. I wanted to be simple and smoky and earthy like the people of the village.

I stacked the extra things in boxes out in the courtyard, never wanting to see them again.

When Gordon came home, he was not quite so impressed with my heaven on earth. He took one look around and headed for the broom. I heard him outside, sweeping up the front steps, washing the droppings of a daylong outdoor picnic down into the gutter sluice that ran into the sea.

I stood dumbly watching him, wanting to tell him what had happened since he left. Then I remembered the suitcases upstairs, still unopened from the night before. The clothes were dirty and would begin to mildew in the heat and dampness. What *had* I done all day?

For one thing, I had not taken Chris swimming as I had promised him. I walked up the stairs looking for him. He was gone. I looked in the boys' room. Nothing but unmade beds stared back. The bathroom was empty except for piles of soggy towels from the beach. Our room was empty, and the three older children out on the balcony sailing paper airplanes had no idea where Chris was. I ran downstairs, then out into the courtyard. It was empty except for the pile of renounced dishes and the stroller that had transported Chris everywhere in the year in America.

The stroller was overturned and covered with the tattered blue blanket that was a part of its equipment. I lifted the blanket, and there sat Chris, his round eyes tearful and his bottom lip pushed out.

"Chris, what are you doing here?"

"I don't like this hotel. I want to go home."

"This is home. This is our house."

He pointed to the kitchen door. "That's not my house," he said angrily. "This is my house." He pulled the blanket back over his head and dismissed me.

I stood, uncertain whether I should let him work it out himself or pick him up and comfort him. I decided to pick him up and comfort him.

"Look, Chris," I said, holding him close. "This *is* our home now. We can't go back!"

"Where is back?" he asked hopefully.

"It's where we can't go, not now. But don't be afraid; Mommy and Daddy are here with you, Chris. We're all together, and wherever we're all together, it's home. Don't be afraid."

I held him gently and felt the fear and indignation go out of his small body. With a yawn and a sleepy sigh, he settled on my shoulder.

"I'll take you swimming tomorrow," I promised.

The next morning Gordon had strung new lines on the balcony overlooking the street, and I stood, properly humbled and domesticated, pinning up clothes while they flapped in the sea breeze.

Across the street on the balcony of the apartment over the wine factory, a young Chinese woman also stood hanging up her wash. I glanced at her a bit guardedly, wondering if she were the mistress now turned respectable wife who had caused the poor woman in the wine factory to hang herself. But in spite of my suspicions, I smiled and nodded.

"Jo-sun, good morning!" I called over the street. "You're washing early!"

"Jo-sun!" she returned civilly, "Why are you doing your own wash? You should have a servant to help you!"

"Why should I?" I called back above the wind. "You don't have a servant!"

"Oh, I am the servant!" she said.

A wet shirt flapped my face, and I ducked.

So, she was not the mistress turned wife who had caused the woman who became the ghost to hang herself. She was the servant.

The shrill voice came back across the wind.

"Why don't you hire a servant?"

"I don't need one," I shouted.

"Ah yah, don't you like Chinese people in your house?"

"Of course I do. We have people in all the time. You can see that for yourself," I said defensively.

"Haih-a. That's true. Then it must be the money."

"Money? What about money?"

"You want to save money. But you know, you shouldn't think about that. Anyone who earns American dollars should be willing to support another family. Maybe you don't need anyone, but other people need work."

I picked up my basket and went inside. The lines were full, and I had had enough of this discussion. With an ability to twist logic like that, she would probably become wife number three.

Before an hour was over, I had walked back to the fish stall to talk to Wong Tai.

"Do you know someone who needs work badly?" I asked.

She pursed her lips and thought for a moment.

"That's a big responsibility, to ask me that. What if she doesn't work out? You might hold it against me."

"No, I wouldn't do that. Do you know someone?"

"Young or old?"

"Well, . . ." I hesitated. "Young enough to work, and old enough not to give me any trouble."

She thought again, pressing her fingers against her teeth. Then her face lighted.

"Ah, I know just the woman for you. She's of middle years, lives in the village, and has children of her own. She's a plain woman but so honest, I'd guarantee her with my own name. When would you want her?"

I thought of the suitcases still full of clothes and the bathtub full of rinse water. "This afternoon?" I asked timidly.

Her eyes widened, and she laughed.

"Ah yah," she corrected me. "No one can come so soon. Maybe next week."

"But I thought she needed work!"

"Face," Wong Tai smiled. "How could she come so quickly and have any self-respect when she talks to you?"

I stumbled back toward the mold-eaten house on the corner, wondering if the brains in this town were run on a different electrical circuit than mine. I must hire someone I had decided not to hire, not because I needed her but because she needed me. And now that I had decided to hire her I could wait for a week, so *I* would be desperate when *she* came instead of the other way around.

And then it dawned on me. What I was bargaining for was not a pound of horse flesh. I was bargaining for the price of someone's self-respect. And it seemed that here loss of self-respect was worse than loss of life. Maybe that was why the woman in the wine factory had hanged herself.

We had finished eating that evening when Wing Sung stopped in.

"My mother invites you all up for dinner," he said politely.

"Ah, that would be nice," Gordon thanked him. "What day would she like us to come?"

Wing looked at him strangely.

"Today," he said, "tonight, up at our house on the hill."

"Oh, I'm sorry. That's too bad . . . I wish we'd known. We've already eaten! Tell your mother thank you, and we're sorry."

Wing was incredulous.

"Seven o'clock, and you've eaten?"

There was an uncomfortable silence.

"Never mind, Dad, we'll go up with him," Marita volunteered. "I love the way Wing cooks."

"Sure, it doesn't matter," Mike agreed. "We can eat again."

"Oh, come on, Dad, let us go. I couldn't find Mei Ho and her sister at the beach today, and they promised a long time ago to teach me how to play mah-jongg."

Wing stood at the door waiting.

"All right," Gordon agreed, "but you've got to be home by nine."

All three children bounded out of the house and followed Wing Sung down the path along the sea, past the Queen of Heaven temple, and up the mountainside to the tangled patchwork of rooftops.

I glanced at Chris, wondering why he had not clamored to go. He was sound asleep on his highchair tray, his red nose testifying that we had made it to the beach.

At nine-thirty, there was no sign of the children. At quarter to ten, the night sounds in the street were unabated. Children called out games under the window, dogs fought, and people laughed. An endless stream of life passed by the house. It was hot and dark, and we began to worry. Had we been careless to let them go?

"Should I take the flashlight and go looking for them?" Gordon asked. I glanced at his face, not being able to tell if he were angry or worried. He could usually sense a situation before he knew the facts.

"Where would you look?" I asked. "Do you know where the Wong's house is?"

"You know, we ate there one night. Where's the flashlight?"

"I don't know. I haven't seen it since we got back."

"I wish you'd get things unpacked and in place."

"I'm trying to. I had to wash and take Chris to the beach today."

We glanced outside, the feeling of impending danger unspoken between us.

"Stay here. I'm going." Gordon said resolutely. I watched him disappear into the night and for the first time, felt alone in the village.

It was after ten-thirty.

The street had become suddenly quiet. The stalls were closed, and everyone was home, eating or sleeping. There was the sound of footfalls outside the window. I peered out and saw the old European coming home from his nightly swim at the far beach, a knapsack over his back. He nodded, bid me "goot effening," and went on up the hillside.

I went outside and looked up the road. Kerosene lights twinkled like low stars on the hillside. Waves slapped lazily against the shore, and a lone dog howled in the distance. On the left over the sea, the farmer's commune clung to the cliffs, looking dark and hostile. The children would have to pass that enemy camp, a camp of people whose little red book taught them not to view us as persons but as imperialist aggressors.

I shivered in the clammy heat and went back into the house to wait.

At ten-forty-five Gordon was back, his eyes big from the darkness and a look of frightened anger.

"I can't find anyone," he said.

I leaned against the wall and started to cry.

He came and put his arms around me, and we stood together.

"I had a feeling we should never have come back here," he said quietly. "If anything happened, it would be all my fault."

It was eleven o'clock, and still no trace of the children. Gordon had the phone in his hand to call the village police when they came bounding in, full of Wing's good cooking and high spirits.

"We had the *best* time!" Deidra laughed. "You should have seen . . ."

She was stopped dead by Gordon's stern face.

"Do you realize what time it is?" he asked, looking at his watch. "You children were supposed to be home by nine!"

The laughter stopped.

"That's stupid," Marita said indignantly. "They hadn't even eaten by nine."

"Yeah, Dad, it really would have been impolite to leave before they ate," Mike agreed. "And they don't have a phone. You see, they fixed all sorts of special stuff for us, and I helped Wing fry fish, and you know, it would have seemed kind of funny for us to leave without eating it."

"Those lucky kids!" Deidra said. "They don't have to go to bed until twelve o'clock. If we are going to be like the village kids, why do we have to go to bed so early?"

Gordon was still looking at his watch, rubbing his wrist.

"Nine o'clock is nine o'clock," he said. "You nearly scared your mother to death. Next time you're home at nine, or you don't go!"

"Okay, then we won't go!" Marita retorted. "You . . . you told us to be friendly and open and take people for what they are, and now you're trying to make us afraid you'll be mad at us when we get home late, even if we have to be impolite. You could at least be *fair!*"

She stamped up the stairs and slammed her bedroom door, and I knew that the disaster *had* happened. It had come, not from any harm intrinsic in the village, but in the confrontation between two lifestyles. And we were caught between the longing to be free and open and the fear of being changed, getting lost.

The children filed solemnly upstairs, and Gordon went out to turn off the front light. I heard him crunching over something on the front steps.

I stood in the doorway, overwhelmed with this torn feeling.

"They were right, you know," I said.

He looked at me as though I had double-crossed him and said nothing.

"We're going to have to be consistent with those kids," I said, "or they'll be so confused they'll withdraw completely."

He looked at me. "What is more consistent than setting standards and demanding that they be met?"

"That's not the way this street operates. That's a different kind of consistency than saying, 'feel free to relate to people, and find out for yourself how it must be done.' What if relating doesn't happen by nine o'clock?"

"You're pretty philosophical, now that they're back in one piece," he said with a small smile.

"But don't you see how silly we were? The fear wasn't out in the street; it was in us! The kids were perfectly safe! We caused the problem by getting scared!"

"The kids caused the problem by not coming home at nine o'clock," he countered. "I still say you have to set standards and stick to them."

"Even if it makes the kids . . . and us . . . feel lonely here?"

He had the broom and was looking for a plastic pail.

"Crabshells!" he said vehemently. "First this sticky mess of red beans and popsicle sticks, and now they're eating *crabs* out here. I swept this off when I came home, and now look at it again!"

"But what do you think we should have done tonight? We let them go and then made them feel guilty."

"Hand me the pail with some water in it, will you?"

"But don't you think we should go up and explain to them?"

"Put some detergent in it too. This place is starting to stink."

"Are you listening to me?"

"Yes, I'm listening. Get a woman turned on to something, and she loses her head. We can find plenty of meaning here without wallowing in garbage or letting things like time schedules go to the winds."

I was standing in the doorway, wondering how much of what he said was true when he set the pail down and laid his arm across my shoulder.

"Come on," he said in a gentler tone. "I do hear you. I suppose there are no simple answers. Let's go talk to the kids. We've got to keep everybody feeling together."

I went with him, sensing for the first time that the word *everybody* was no longer confined to these six people. In some way, the word *everybody* had begun to mean the children who sat on the steps, the people in the market and on the hill, and yet in that huge web of everybodiness, these six were still the most important. To hurt them would be to hurt everybody.

It was a week to the day when Fong Oi knocked on the door. I opened it, and she stepped in confidently. She was a short woman in her middle forties, plumpish, with a shy smile, a soft voice, and gold-edged teeth. She was dressed in a grey cotton sam-fu and carried a plastic shopping bag.

"Wong Tai tells me you're inviting someone to work for you?"

"Haih-a, Right! Please come in and sit, ah, what is your honorable name?"

"My small surname is Fong. You may call me Wai."

I paused, puzzled, not able to make the connection between the words. Surely my Chinese was not that deficient.

"Ah Wai, Fong Wai, is that your full name?"

She looked shyly at the floor and smiled, as though unable to lie and embarrassed to tell the truth.

"I have a strange name," she confessed. "When I was born, my mother called me Fong Oi, Love Fong, as you would say it. But how can I ask you to call me Love? Ah, Love, sweep the floor, Love, wash the dishes. Ah yah! I'd die laughing! It's too private a name for such use. Better to call me Fong Person, Fong Wai . . . Ah Wai will do."

I felt strangely intimidated by this person I had been asked to hire.

"Whatever you say. You can call me Mrs. Ding . . . Ding Tai."

"I'll call you Missy."

"Ah yah, don't call me Missy! I hate that! All my Chinese friends call me Ding Tai."

"You must not confuse friends and servants," she said softly. "You call me Ah Wai, I'll call you Missy. Now what is the work you want me to do?"

Days followed days in hot steamy succession. Our children lived at the beach, lost their white look, and became as brown and lean as the village children. Gordon was busy at school, interviewing students and setting up a fall schedule, and with the coming of Ah Wai, I had more time to spend at the beach with the children and to wander through the village looking and listening. There was time to think about the whole dynamic of what was happening and to keep my ears open for the first stirrings of the Eighth Month Festival which we had heard of before but had never experienced from the *inside*. I felt somehow compelled to listen to everything I could in the village, to jot it down in a black notebook, and try to understand the pattern it was forming.

But when Gordon came home in the evening, he longed for peace and quiet. And if there were one thing the house on the corner was not, it was quiet. The windows along the sides of the living room opened out directly over the street. Passers-by could lean in and bid us the time of the day, and sometimes did. Small boys threw pebbles in to hear them skip across the tile floor, and friends waved to us while we ate our meals. It was not exactly what one would call private.

"Remember, it was your idea to move here!" I teased Gordon, but he looked at me and smiled half-heartedly, as though that were a stale joke by now.

One day Gordon came home with a pile of wooden shutters.

"What on earth are those for?" I asked.

"I'm going to get Chun Sang the carpenter to make a frame and fasten them along the bottom of the living room windows."

"But what about the feeling of openness, of being a part of life as it passes this corner?"

"I'm all for openness, you know that, but this gets ridiculous. Someone from the commune spat in here the other morning when I was reading the paper, and I'm not taking that!"

"When? You didn't tell me about it."

I saw a rare anger, rising on his usually calm face.

"Tell you? I didn't want to tell you. You would have given me that same look you give me every time I pick up a broom . . . that *oh, you insensitive Pharisee* look . . . like I have some sort of hormone imbalance or psychological hangup about cleanliness, like I'm abnormal because I don't want to walk on spit and crabshells."

I felt as if he had punched me in the stomach.

"And I suppose you think *I'm* growing horns and a moustache because I don't want to live behind dark brown shutters!" I struck back, "If you put those up, it's going to feel like a prison in here. I like the wind blowing through the house. I want it *open!*"

He stacked the shutters in the corner and sighed, his face composed again.

"You've changed," he said sadly. "Do you remember the first day I showed you this house, and you refused to live here until I promised to put up a brass rod all around the windows for drapes, so it would be private?"

He looked so forlorn I had to comfort him, like Chris under the stroller.

"You changed me," I said quietly. "You changed me from someone who was afraid of everything to someone who wants to *know* everything. Aren't you happy with what you've created?"

"I don't know," he said, softly kissing my cheek. "Aren't there some things we should be afraid of? Aren't there some lines that shouldn't be crossed? Where does all this end?"

I helped him stack the shutters, wondering what was happening. What was this brakes-on attitude? Was it some new kind of leadership, leading by stepping behind? Who was behind and who was ahead in this crazy dance, or were we going around in circles?

"If I thought you knew what you were doing," I said, "I'd relax and let you do it. But if you're running, I'm not going to follow you."

His look made me sorry I had spoken so brashly.

"I wouldn't claim to know what I'm doing," he said gently. "But I do know it feels right in relationship to what *you're* doing. Do you know what you're doing?"

"I'm just trying to feel free."

"From me?" he asked.

"No, silly. Just inside myself."

"I'd like to feel free too. I'd like to feel free to pick up a broom when I feel like it without having you look at me like that."

"Okay, I promise. Just don't make *me* feel guilty when you do it."

"Why should you feel guilty?" he asked. "You're not even responsible for the sweeping anymore."

I hadn't thought of that, and when I did think of it, I wasn't sure I liked it.

Late one afternoon after the shutters had been properly installed, the little Lu girl came in with her baby brother tied on her back. She eyed the shutters warily.

"What are those?" she asked.

"Gates to close up the bottom of the window."

"But why?"

"When we eat, we don't like everyone looking in at us."

"But why?" she asked. "Everyone looks at *us* when *we* eat!"

I thought of the market street, of the folding tables set up in front of stalls at noon where one ate and waved to the passers-by in a spirit of sidewalk cafe. Before I could find an answer she looked up at me and asked penetratingly, "Do foreigners do something *strange* when they eat? Why don't you want anyone to see you?"

The sluggish days of August moved over the village. There was not a breath of wind from the warm littered sea. The odor of fish drying on the beach hung over the street like a pall. The village children sat on the steps in greater numbers than ever, eating and playing ten-cent gambling games, reading Chinese comics and tumbling over each other. By the time Gordon came home at night, the front steps usually looked like a battleground.

Sometimes Gordon could surreptitiously find the broom and sweep the steps without causing any trouble, and I conscientiously looked the other way, figuring the broom was now in other hands. But one day, Wong Tai was passing while he was doing his sweeping. She shook her head.

"Ah yah, Ding Sang. You're a headmaster. You shouldn't be out here waving a broom like a common street sweeper. Where's that lazy servant I sent you?"

He turned and saw Ah Wai standing in the open door, her face a deep red. What chance did a man have to be free in a world where women controlled the brooms?

It was a Saturday afternoon when the crabshell issue was finally resolved, as much as issues like that are ever resolved.

We had decided to build a low brick wall inside the courtyard and fill it with soil so we could plant a small vegetable garden close to the kitchen. The vegetables in the market were good for cooking and for making Chinese food, but they were all grown with nightsoil for fertilizer and were not safe to eat raw in salads. Vegetables that could be peeled, such as cucumbers and carrots, could still be eaten raw, but we were hungry for fresh green lettuce.

Tommy and Wing Sung had promised to come and help us that weekend, and soon after lunchtime they came, dragging a bag of cement, a mixing trough, and trowels in through the orange courtyard door.

Along with the two teenagers came a new friend, Tong. Tong was older than the other boys, perhaps twenty-three or twenty-four, tall, muscular, with the smooth sensitive face and large eyes of an ivory carving. He spoke some English but was relieved to know he could speak in Chinese and be understood as well. Gordon had met him in his wanderings about the village, but I had never seen him before.

"You should talk with Tong sometime," he said. "He's an artist and a philosopher. He has some very interesting ideas."

Tong held up his hand modestly.

"No, No!" He laughed. "You must not call me an artist or a philosopher. I'm only a poor uneducated man who likes to think. If I have any art, it has grown out of my thinking. Sometimes I make pictures of the village, but I don't always paint what I see; sometimes I paint what I think. You may not like it at all."

I looked at him, tall and bronzed like a polished statue, and wondered what these things he thought were that we might not like at all. In a way he seemed more threatening than the younger more compliant friends we had made in the village. Beneath his smooth exterior, there was a wild animal quality, a tremendous vitality.

Gordon and the others mixed the cement and worked in the open courtyard, laying the bricks in a long L shape, forming a box against two existing walls. The sun beat down on their bare backs, sending trickles of perspiration down their brown bodies and across their faces.

"Ah yah," Wing Sung breathed. "I'm going over to the wine factory and take a shower when I'm done here."

"You'd better go before dark," Tommy teased him. "You know the ghost in the wine factory comes out after dark. I saw it the other night, two big green eyes glowing in the dark."

"Aren't those gas jets under the mash?" I asked.

"Wing believes in ghosts," Tommy said, laughing.

"How about you, Tong," said Gordon. "Do you believe in ghosts?"

"Ghosts, devils, spirits, they are all a part of our tradition," Tong said. "And I personally neither believe nor disbelieve in them. I try to observe what is happening, and how people are affected by their beliefs. Are you interested in this kind of thing?"

"The Devil Festival!" Wing said excitedly before Gordon could answer. "You and Ding Tai must go this year to the Devil Festival. It's one of the most important . . ."

"Devil Festival," Tommy said disgustedly. "Do you know the old men of the Kai Fong spend ten thousand dollars a year on a festival like that? And yet when a group of us went to them and asked them for a youth center, they turned their heads and said there was no money . . . no money!"

"It's not all the money," defended Wing, whose father was a leader in the Kai Fong community association. "Some of the family heads think that a youth center is a dangerous thing. They say that it's bad for the youth to group together away from their families. They say this is where the mischief starts, with each *hau-sang-ji* trying to act bigger than the others away from the influence of the elders."

"But this Ghost Festival, this Devil Festival," I asked, "what is it about? What does it mean?"

Tong laid down his trowel and smiled.

"Ayie, how could I tell you, just like that, standing in this courtyard. You must be there, standing in the firelight and hearing the drums; you must find the meaning yourself."

I wanted to ask him more, but Tommy interrupted, bored with ghosts.

"What are you going to plant in this garden?" he asked.

At the same moment Gordon and I looked at each other. With Tommy's mother selling vegetables in the market, how could we politely explain ourselves?

"Plants," I stammered. "We're going to plant, uh, all sorts of things here!"

"I have a papaya tree," Tong offered. "And some beautiful wild plants from the mountainside."

Tommy and Wing offered plants as well, and that afternoon, what we had planned to become a private lettuce garden became a Friendship Garden with each plant a reminder of its donor. Again the village had bent us to its shape.

Before the boys went home, Gordon brought up the problem of the front steps.

"You fellows sound like good solid advisors," he said. "What can we do about the village children sitting on our doorstep?"

They looked at each other and dropped their eyes.

"Why is that a problem?" Tong asked. "We all sat there."

"I don't mind the children *sitting* there, but it's the garbage. They throw garbage all over the steps."

A glance passed among the boys and a moment of pained silence.

"You could put a garbage can by the front door," someone began.

"You could put electric wiring under your welcome mat—"

"You could put up an iron gate and only give the key to your own family members—"

"No, no, no! We wouldn't do that!"

"You could chase them away with a big stick like the man who used to live in this house. The way they knew he was dead one day was that he didn't come out with his stick."

The discussion went on for half an hour surmising whether the old man's spirit was still living in the house and proposing remedies, each person's suggestions topping the others in brutality or cleverness. Finally someone came up with the winning suggestion.

"Dump a pail of water on the steps every hour. It will be too wet to sit on, and very clean!"

There was a burst of nervous laughter from the boys, and Tommy stuck his thumb up sharply to indicate that this was the number one idea. There was a strange gleam in his usually merry eyes, and he waited until it was quiet before he spoke.

"Ah ha!" he said. "We have defeated the enemy!"

The word *enemy* hung in the air like an explosive. Had the children on the steps become our enemy? Did a clean doorstep mean more to us than a sense of community, of give and take?

That night I stood in the doorway, pushing the red remains of a crab with my bare toe. It felt hard and dead. What was it about these harmless objects that was causing such uneasiness in our household? Was it the annoyance of the shells themselves, or had they become symbols of an invisible fear, the fear of the deep intrusion the village was making into our way of life? Was it the ingrained connection between cleanliness and godliness that was bothering us? No, it was more *of the spirit* than that.

I stood gazing at the shells, knowing I should get the broom and sweep them into the gutter since it was Ah Wai's day off, yet something stopped me. There was a fear, the fear of pushing people away, of making a clean place and dying alone inside it without ever catching the secret of this street, and yet there was another fear, a counter fear, (or was it a counter-counter fear?) of *emptying myself,* of becoming something else when I did not yet know what that something else would be. If life were not regulated by the clock and the broom and the dark brown shutters, what would come in their place? The words *emptied himself* echoed hauntingly around the edges of my mind . . . calling like a distant entrancing wind.

The sea pounded and slapped on the beach, and I felt pulled, as though by the force of the tide, from everything small and comfortable I had ever known to something wild and untamed . . . from every simple yes and no to an area of complexity that was staggering.

I felt a hand on my shoulder and jumped, my nerves on edge.

It was Gordon, going out of the door to sweep the steps. Strangely, I felt comforted.

"Just once a day," he said. "They'll need a clean place to sit in the morning."

the devil festival

For several days, an electrifying shiver of excitement had been building on the hot village streets. Between the baskets of green vegetables in the market, bright colored paper boats were being constructed on wooden frames. On the winding shady street that ran past the rice shop, red and yellow crepe houses bloomed like giant flowers while round white paper lanterns dangled in dark corners, waiting to be lit.

Occasionally the pounding of drums could be heard from the Tin-Hau temple by the sea, and the sound of gongs preceded the frequent processions that wound through the streets. Groups of preadolescent boys, garbed in blue and gold jackets, solemnly carried wooden swords from the temple. Dignified men in red capes and black caps led processions of older boys carrying banners. It was as though the village were preparing for some eventuality, some somber reality, and it must dress in bright colors and prepare the way with gongs and drums.

In the market there was a strange mixture of gaiety and grimness as the adults prepared to celebrate the inevitable *presence of evil* and the children anticipated the prospect of ghosts, devils, and treats.

I walked down the street on my way to the Store and passed Yau Tai, busy stuffing paper bank notes into a worn grey basket. This morning preparing for the festival, her usually jolly face was agitated. She looked flustered from the heat and embarrassed by my presence, as if I had taught her son to be an unbeliever. She glanced at me absently, preoccupied, talking to herself as much as to me.

"Ah, Ding Tai, they won't help me get ready. First Tommy, and now son number two says he doesn't believe in it. Says it's for old women and fools. Wouldn't that kill you? Do you know what their father would say if he were here? Ah yah, he'd beat them to death. Very believing, he is. Ah."

She began stuffing the imitation paper money in the basket again mumbling to herself, "But of course he's not here, of course."

"Haih-a," I agreed. "I guess that doesn't help the boys' attitude."

She seemed lost in her anxious thoughts, and I moved on, respecting her right to privacy even though she had no door to shut.

I went up the stone steps and into the Store. Here there were no signs of the ghosts and devils of the festival. The store was neatly arranged with shelves and counters, a freezer, and soft-drink signs. Mr. Hong, the owner, stood behind the wooden counter peering out at me through his thick glasses as he always did. To him, the festival was a thing of the past. His ghosts and devils were the colonialists and imperialist aggressors who had invaded and prostituted China, and he had no time for a superstitious tradition like the Devil Festival or anyone who was a direct descendant of his particular brand of devils, especially Americans.

Curious, I thought as I watched him figure up the bill on his abacus, that he would even deign to import Western goods and sell them to those he despised so. But then, as Tommy had explained to us, the villagers were practical people and had learned to eat pig dung, when it was necessary, to live.

I went out of the store and into the rush of the street. Housewives bustled elbow to elbow, and fishermen squeezed through the press of bodies, their black oily garments ripe with the smell of the sea. By the fruit stand next to Yau Tai, a woman bartered for oranges to be used in the festival.

"These are good!" the man in the stall said. "Sweet, juicy, ah, these are the best!" He picked up a long knife and slashed the fruit open for her to taste.

She sucked the orange and looked doubtful.

"Ah yah," she said, "no need for such good ones. They're only for the worship of the spirits. Do you have something a little cheaper?"

Down the shady rice-shop street in the odds-and-ends shop, the young woman's eyes were pools of suffering. Three bright healthy tots played on the floor of the shop, but in a box behind the counter lay a listless, emaciated baby.

I saw the child move jerkily. Its tiny legs and arms were like dried twigs and its face had the shrunken look of an old woman.

The sad-eyed woman came to wait on me. She glanced at the baby, and our eyes met.

"Do you have enough food for the baby?" I asked, wondering if the question might offend her.

"She won't eat, Ding Tai. She never cries or makes any trouble, but she won't eat."

"Do you have anything for her besides milk?"

"She eats a little soft rice."

"How old is she?"

"Not quite a year. She was born after the Devil Festival last year."

"Have you tried baby foods?"

"Ah, I know you Siyan have good methods of raising babies, but that isn't the problem. I have three good children, but this one . . . this one . . ."

The dark pools of her eyes filled with tears, and she leaned over the counter speaking softly. "Ding Tai, this one causes me much pain in my mind. My three children were only a year apart, and you know how men are. My husband didn't want me to get something to stop the babies. He thinks the more babies I have the more man he is. And when I knew I would have this one, I wanted to die, to die of the weariness. So I went to an herb doctor for medicine, wanting to make it drop before it was too big. But, ah yah—" the tears escaped from the brown pools and coursed down her cheeks, "—it didn't drop out. The herbs only half-killed it. It was born with something wrong. Its brain is ruined. *Ayie,* I did this to my own child; I wish I had died."

The tears were contagious. I found myself looking at her, wanting to tell her I knew what she was suffering, but I knew she was alone in her pain, alone in a way I could not reach her.

"Have you taken her to the doctor?" I asked for lack of anything else to say.

"Haih, I took her to the Western Medicine Clinic soon after she was born. I told the doctor, but he didn't understand. They don't understand us and our medicines. He said one baby in every so many is born like this, that the abortion herbs had nothing to do with it, but I know it did. I know I did this to my own child. Ayie!"

I passed the wine factory walls and went through the narrow tunnel where the smell of sour mash was so intense, it overwhelmed my senses. Down at the temple by the sea where the image of the King of Evil was being built, the sound of pounding could be heard. The air of suspense was pounding through the streets, the sea was pounding on the beach . . . pounding, pounding through the air, through my mind.

I glanced into the dark doorway of the wine factory as I passed and wondered how they would cope with their ghost. For a moment I caught my steps quickening and my heart beating faster. She seemed almost real.

The morning of the festival, the excitement exploded into visible images in the village. This was the day, and it was to be celebrated with the boom of drums and the clang of gongs.

The boys in the blue jackets marched in the opening procession, led by the red-robed officials and followed by the image of the Queen of Heaven ensconced in a sedan chair and festooned by fruits and buns. Young men carrying elaborately decorated swords from the temple formed the honor guard.

Booming and clanging, the procession wound its way down the market street. At every home, the women laid out oranges and burned fragrant sandalwood sticks. The air was tense. The good goddess must be pleased, so she would help the villagers that night in their confrontation with the powers of evil.

We stood in the house on the corner watching the processions go by. Ah Wai padded through the house, her soft slippers making a swishing sound on the earthen tile floor. She occasionally glanced out the window commenting on the proceedings, their cost, and whether they were well performed or not.

A group of men passed the window carrying a cage with two birds in it. Behind them moved a crowd of village children cheering, shouting and eating popsicles.

"Why the birds in the cage?" I asked, wondering if they would be killed for sacrifice or some blood-letting ritual of atonement.

"Ah, they will take them to the other end of the beach and let them go," she said "They open the cage and let the birds fly, like freeing the spirits of people. When the birds fly up, we all see ourselves go free. Who doesn't dream of being free?" She sighed and looked vacantly out of the window.

I watched her flap the dust rag in the air like a broken wing and felt guilty.

"Do you feel free?" I asked.

"No one is completely free," she said. "It's only a hope people have."

"Did you tell me you were born in Mainland China?"

"Haih," she said, without raising her eyes.

"Did you run from China to find freedom?" I asked.

She looked at me incredulously, as if I had asked her if the stork actually brought babies.

"How could anything be that simple?" She laughed. "No, I came to Hong Kong because I had to. My husband needed me."

"Why was he here without you?"

She sighed again and flipped the dust rag, resettling all the dust, and scooted across the floor wearily. "Ah yah," she said. "It's too long a story to tell you now. Sometime when there isn't so much work to do. I'd like to get through in time to watch the Jit-Mok tonight."

"You can leave anytime you need to," I said. "Do you want to go home and get ready now?"

She smiled her slow, dry smile, with a touch of shyness.

"Ah," she said, "I don't have too much to get ready. I won't burn money or houses, I only like to sit by the fires and visit with friends. I've seen too many kinds of devils to fear any one kind. Japanese soldiers beheaded my mother. When the Communists came, the devils were the rich; here in Hong Kong, the devils are the poor. When I go to the school where my sons study, I see they fear the Western Devil, and they teach my sons to stay away from these festivals. But I say, what's the difference? Fear one devil and you fear them all! Hah! I've seen too many kinds of devils to fear any of them. With my luck, I couldn't die even if I tried." And she flip-flopped across the floor, shaking what was left of the dust back onto the tiles where it settled in dismal flecks.

When the last procession began its booming way through the streets, it was already dusk. In front of every house and shop a small sandbank had been heaped, and into this was stuck the smoking heung, bowl of fruit, cooked noodles, and at some places even a cup of tea with rice, chopsticks, and cooked vegetables.

Gordon, the children, and I stood by our front door until the procession passed. Then we followed it past the banyan tree and the Chun's shop, where Chun Tai nervously put out oranges. At the Wongs' fish market, Wong Tai spread out cooked noodles, and a shower of coins fell from her hands and clattered onto the pavement.

Out of the dusky shadows children appeared, swooping up the coins as fast as they hit the ground. In a moment all that was left was the patter of small, bare feet as they followed the procession.

I looked at Wong Tai, who smiled back unperturbed.

"Are the children supposed to do that?" I asked her anxiously.

She smiled at me and winked.

"Who did you expect to take the money?" she asked. "The ghosts?"

Before too many minutes our three eldest had caught on and were lost in the grey shadows of the streets, playing ghost and swooping up coins.

We followed the procession around the loop of the village, the drums shattering all attempts at conversation. At each home, women came and laid out food and incense and money in the doorway. Sometimes at houses where we were not known, our presence caused women to stare at our faces and draw back and exclaim, "Ah yah, yauh gwai, there are devils." Some who knew us would say, "Don't fear, that's just the Dings. They're harmless."

At the door of the wine factory apartment, wife number two laid out oranges, tea, and rice for the ghost of wife number one while the servant looked over her shoulder with a gleam in her eye. For the first time I felt sorry for the mistress turned wife, now caught between the ghost and the servant.

It was dark, and the warm sea lapped lazily on the beach. The sky was overcast, and a hot wind swirled the dust in gnatlike eddies. From every section of the village, groups of men, women and children were coming, passing the house on the corner on their way to the temple by the sea.

Someone knocked on the door, and China Pearl, Tommy, and Wing came in, ready to take us to the ceremony. Their faces were tense, and even Tommy who disclaimed the whole procedure was chatting excitedly in spite of himself.

"Have you seen the Bad King?" he asked. "They've got him all built, out of paper and wood."

"You can see him burned tonight," Wing added. "Maybe even more than once."

They laughed at this, and I felt the loneliness of standing among those who are joking when I did not know the prior fact the joke was built on. I glanced at Gordon, and he was out of it as well, which felt at least a little better . . . perhaps he was right . . . perhaps we were strangers here, if strangers could be defined as those who did not understand the jokes.

Gordon tossed Chris up on his shoulders, and we followed the teenagers out the door and along the sea path to the temple of the Queen of Heaven. Small fires had now appeared in the darkness along the beach, and the slow rhythmic beating of a gong sounded in the night air.

"Where's Tong?" Gordon asked. "I thought he was coming tonight."

"He'll be here later," Tommy said, trying to walk next to Pearl. "He works for an English bachelor and doesn't get off work until late tonight."

"I didn't know that's what he did," Gordon said. "He never told me about that; he said he sells his paintings."

The boys laughed.

"Ah, maybe the man does promise to buy a few of his paintings too," said Wing. "But you can't make a living being an artist. Even artists have to eat a little pig dung once in a while."

"Don't worry, Tong will be here," Tommy promised. "This is one festival he seems to need."

"Haih," laughed Wing. "Tong has many ghosts, many mistakes to be made right. He even told me one time he feels like there are devils—"

"—in him?" Tommy laughed. "Did he tell you that too? Ah yah, you can't take Tong too seriously. He thinks he has gods inside him too. He's a little *chi-sin!*" And Tommy tapped his head, to be sure the meaning was plain to us.

The pink front of the temple with its white carved lions was barely visible in the darkness, but the fragrance of the coiled incense burning inside was even heavier than the odor from the pig lots on the hillsides. The flat grassy area from the temple to the sea was dotted with small fires, and leering above the fires towered the image of Wan Lo, the King of Evil, the god of the underworld. His twenty-foot frame was covered with gaudily colored scrap paper flapping in the wind like scales, and the eyes in his hideous face glared neon red in the blackness. Around his feet the small fires leapt and twisted, casting weird shadows on the gigantic effigy.

The beach and the grass were covered with a crowd of all ages. In the center of the crowd, two tables were heaped with pink buns filled with sweet soybean paste and cone-shaped piles of oranges. On top of the buns a stiff white pair of hands stretched out, looking ghostly in the darkness. The firelight flickered making them seem to move.

At the end of one table, the officials sat, the performers of the ritual. The most prominent was a priest in fancy headdress. Four men assisted him, two on either side of the table. The man in the headdress read from a large book of scriptures in a monotone while one of the assistants banged on a gong, making it impossible to hear.

The crowd was quiet. Men and women sat in small clumps, speaking in murmurs. I saw Ah Wai sitting with her husband, her three sons, and her daughter. She looked different here, somehow more self-assured, more relaxed, somehow deeply fresh and innocent. In the flickering fires to the right, Yau Tai was seriously burning her paper money to the spirits, and closer to the center sat the sad-eyed young woman with the limp bundle tied to her back. Even the three energetic toddlers were quiet, waiting for the moment three or four hours away when the King of Evil would be burned and the treats could be eaten in celebration.

A flare of light flashed up behind the huge image, and a murmur rose from the crowd. Two men rushed to the fire and began beating it out. The murmur died down.

Tommy glanced at Wing.

"Who's doing it this year?" he asked.

"The Jeng boys," Wing said. He was quiet, so quiet and different from the Wing we had known last year I hardly felt I recognized him. Then he had been questing, inquisitive; now he seemed to have settled into a dull kind of acceptance. Even tonight, there was a difference between him and Tommy. Tommy, who thoroughly doubted the worth of the whole procedure, was at least articulate about its meaning. Wing merely accepted it as a process and had little to say about it, or if he did say something, it was a simple recitation of facts with little understanding on his part of what they might mean outside his particular cultural group.

"What are they doing?" I heard Gordon asking.

"Every year we play a kind of game," Tommy explained. "The men build the statue and try to protect it until the right time to burn it, and the young boys always try to sneak up behind the Bad King and burn it before it is time. It's a kind of thing we act out."

So that was the missing fact the joke had been built on—there was a ritualized expression of the elders as keepers of tradition and youth as the challengers of tradition.

"Only every year we act it out, it gets more real to me," Tommy said. "The Kai Fong spends thousands of dollars for this night, hiring the priests, buying the food and costumes, and yet they refuse to think of starting a scholarship fund for the young people of the village."

"The letter is gone from the Evil King's hand," China Pearl said. "Do you know who got it this year?"

"Somebody from one of the fishing boats," Tommy said with disgust. "And what good will it do? It's another superstition," he explained to us, "there is a large letter in the Bad King's hand, and if any father takes it without the priest's seeing him and gives it to his son, the son is supposed to grow up to be a great scholar. I suppose the Kai Fong thinks this is their contribution to education, and scholarships aren't necessary. Put a little good luck symbol in an envelope, and some lucky boy will pass the government exams. Hah!" Tommy cleared his throat and spat on the ground, and Wing moved away from him.

The Jeng boys sneaked around the back of the temple and joined our group, looking like boyish versions of Pearl. Both of the eldest boys were there, flashing bright smiles of youthful triumph and smelling like fire. Wing slapped the young Jengs on the back, and the three of them stood arm in arm, the firm believers.

The gongs were beating faster now, and our children stood in the leaping firelight, watching the sights and sounds. Young boys dug more trenches around the base of the image, burning paper money, clothing, houses, and boats. One pink and yellow building stood out in the firelight unburned with the Chinese characters for Male and Female marked on it.

"What is that for?" Gordon asked.

"Just what it looks like," Wing replied deadpan, "Toilets for the men and women ghosts. Can you imagine how angry they would be if they came here tonight and we forgot?"

I glanced at him, wondering if he were serious or joking. But he was dead serious.

Tong burst into the circle of firelight, his face red and puffed. He strode into the middle of the circle, picked up three buns from the ceremonial table and began to eat. Some of the smaller children gasped and pointed, but the rest looked the other way.

"I thought no one was supposed to eat the buns yet," Marita said.

"Ah, that's Tong," Tommy smiled. "He's an artist. No one expects an artist to act in the usual way. Let him."

Tong came and stood with us, the smell of rice wine strong on his breath. He leaned his hand on Gordon's shoulder and smiled, his teeth white and his smooth face drawn tight.

When he spoke, his words sounded strange, as though they came from somewhere outside him.

"This festival, I like . . ." he said thickly, "I like to open it all up . . . it feels good, you know, how good it feels when you look it in the face? Haih, all those dark shadows—see all those dark shadows? And then you light a fire and open up your arms, and you tell them . . . you tell the dark shadows, come on and dance with me, Ah yah, dance with me while I look into your face and laugh, and then go, and leave me alone . . . *alone* . . ."

He was suddenly quiet, with the last word "*alone*" spoken in a low moan. I glanced at him and saw a look of wild fright in his eyes. Gordon put his arm around Tong's shoulders and gripped him tightly, while the others stood in silence.

The breeze from the sea bent the fires shoreward and rattled the strips of white paper lanterns strung overhead. I looked up and asked what they were for.

"Each family has one," Tommy explained, "and that is the family name written on it, asking to be excused for the mistakes they made this year and saying they gave money to the festival."

"But why can't they ask each other's pardon, instead of doing it that way?"

"Ah, face. It is easier to ask the gods for pardon than to ask each other. And then there are the mistakes that are made without knowing. Everything, known and unknown, must be cleared up tonight."

"What are the hands above the table?" I asked Wing.

"For the ghosts to take the buns." he said matter-of-factly. I waited for him to say something I could identify with, something that would help me translate it out of his culture and into mine, but he did not seem to know how to do this. He sensed I was waiting, but all he said was, "Ghosts have no hands." I did not find that particularly enlightening.

"Is this clearing up of everything the basic meaning of the festival?" Gordon asked. "What would you say is its true meaning?"

The boys looked at each other. The Jeng boys laughed and shook their heads. Wing spread his palms and said, "We just celebrate it. We don't stop and think of its meaning." Tommy cocked his head and looked objective, like a critical observer.

"That's a big question, which could take all night to answer," he began. "But maybe I can explain it simply to you like this. The people think there is an evil power, there are ghosts, and there is some hell-power that will get them if they don't make it happy. So they call on the kind goddess, the Heaven Queen, to protect them from the evil and forgive their mistakes. Oh, and there is a Big Judge too, and they ask him to be kind and not judge too harshly, and then they give all the gods and devils money so they will be happy and leave the people alone for a year."

I stood staring at the wind-fanned fires listening to Tommy's voice and wondering how the idea had ever come to the villagers that their everyday dealings with each other in this primitive place were somehow an offense against the gods, that there was a connection . . . forgive us our debts as we forgive our debtors. . . .

Tong was eating the pink buns, sobered a bit by the starchy food.

"That is the way a child would explain the festival," he said turning to Tommy. "To me the meaning is much different. It is not a matter of pleasing the good goddesses and the bad devils. It is a matter of daring to look at the fears, of saying, 'Come, I will make a paper image of you and burn you to the ground and dance in the light of your fire.' It is one night when you know the dead are not dead . . . that all around us float the spirits of those who have lived, have ever lived, the things that have been done . . . that our minds are made up even of these things and these people . . . nothing ever done is completely undone . . . even if the gods be pleased with gifts . . . but you must learn to dance with it . . . Ayie! You must not explain this festival too easily or you will only despise it!"

Tommy looked at Tong as though this were the sort of nonsense one might expect of a drunken artist. He smiled knowingly at us and swept his hand toward the fires, the image, the gongs, and the chanting.

"Isn't this a strange sight in a civilized world?" he asked.

I shot a sideways glance at him and caught a wistfulness on his face, as if deep within himself he wished it did some meaning for him and that he could believe what for him was no longer possible or credible.

"What *do* you believe in?" I asked.

His face made a quick change to the bright impish smile.

"I believe in myself!" he said jauntily. "Most of us have been educated now. We don't need a belief in any gods."

"Then this ceremony is without meaning for you?"

"Haih," he grinned, "if you're not afraid of the devils, then you don't need a god to protect you, do you? I believe in myself, and need neither."

It was still hours until the image would be burned. The children were getting sleepy and restless, and Chris had fallen asleep in Gordon's arms. Tong wanted to stay and see the image burned, but Tommy, Wing, and the Jengs walked back with us.

They led us back on the path between the temple and the sea, over the bridge and through the trees to where the road came to the edge of the beach. Here the street lights half dispelled the inky darkness. Beside the road a small stone structure squatted beneath a natural round boulder.

"What is this used for?" I asked Tommy, who seemed to have the best grasp on simple answers.

"That is the shrine to the earth god," he said. "For almost two hundred years the people of the village have burned heung here, so the earth god will protect the territory."

"But what is this?" Gordon asked, picking up a heavy book tied to the shrine by a chain.

"That is the report book of the policemen. Now the policemen have taken over the work of the earth god. They patrol this area of the beach and write an hourly report in the book." He smiled in his impish way. "The work of the gods is being taken over by men!"

Beside the report book on the stone surface, there were piles of crushed sandalwood ash, and on the left, two fragrant sticks smoldered, their grey smoke making silent spirals in the half-illumined darkness.

"Then what are those?" Gordon asked.

"The policemen can't take care of everything," injected China Pearl, coming out of her quietness. "The policemen may wear the uniform of the gods, but they can be even more evil than ordinary men with all that power, and the bribes."

"And the crops?" added Wing. "Who will make sure that the crops will grow on the hillside? Who will watch over floods and storms? Ah yah, better to burn a few heung beside the report book so all things are tended to."

Tommy was silent, and in the distance the gongs boomed like an eerie heartbeat in the night.

When we tucked the children in bed, they were still impressed by the festival.

"But we always have to leave before the *good* stuff happens," Marita complained. "Why are you guys always in such a hurry? Why couldn't we wait to see that thing burned and eat the buns?"

"That was sort of like halloween," Mike said sleepily. "Playing ghosts and stuff. I got almost a dollar. Do you need it for anything, Mom?"

"No, you can keep it," I said. "That's half the fun."

DeDe looked up at me with big eyes.

"I was wondering," she asked solemnly. "Is it right for American kids to keep money that's been given to Chinese ghosts?"

I pinched her toe under the sheet. "Ah, I guess we're all pretty much the same by the time we get stripped down to the ghost stage."

She looked relieved.

"Next year can we stay until they eat the buns?" Marita persisted.

"Maybe," I promised. "We'll see."

Next year.

Gordon and I went up to the small white room on the third floor, the room with the balcony overlooking the sea. It was late, and the noises of the gongs and the chanting sounded far away and impossible.

It was hot. The sheets felt clammy, and the sea sounded so close I was sure with every roar it would come crashing in through the open windows.

"What was going on with Tong tonight?" I asked.

"He was just a little under—"

"But he seemed to be speaking out of some sort of trance state. I don't know if it was the drink or his mental problems or what, but he seemed to be speaking out of a level that was so much deeper than simply standing for or rebelling against customs like the others. He was using the cultural symbols, but what he said was fascinating. Where does he get those ideas?"

"I don't know. He's different. Did I ever tell you about Tong?"

"What about him?"

"Tong grew up without a father. He had one, I hear, until he was about five, and then his father was killed in a boat accident. His mother was a fisherwoman and had no way of earning enough money to send him to school—I think he went for two or three years—so what he's learned beside reading and writing, he's mostly taught himself."

"Maybe that's why he's so creative. He never had to beat off some killing educational system."

"Could be. It doesn't always work that way though. Tong is an extremely sensitive guy, and with his lack of education, I can see how having to work as a houseboy for a living would bother him."

We were perspiring so much it felt terrible even to touch hands. The gongs made a kind of nightmare sound above the crash of the beach.

"And that isn't the worst of it," Gordon said sleepily. "I heard from the other boys that Tong was engaged to be married. Since it was tough on him to earn the money for a dowry, he signed himself up on a merchant ship, planning to be married when he got back. But two years later when his ship came back, his girl friend met him at the pier with a baby . . . hers by someone else. The girl's momma had been sure Tong would jump ship in some foreign country and never come back, so she gave her daughter to some other fellow."

"Just like a piece of property? Didn't she have anything to say about it?"

"Well I guess that was part of the problem. The girl liked them both, Tong and this other fellow, and when he was gone for a while, momma gave a shove in the other direction."

"How terrible! What did he do?"

"What could he do? They say he lost his head for a few days, went completely berserk. He went to a bar in Wanchai, got drunk, and beat up a prostitute until she nearly died. They say he was in such a state of shock he nearly lost his mind."

I thought of tall, beautiful Tong, the carved ivory statue with the big eyes and the smooth face, standing in the firelight, dancing in his imagination with his fears and guilts; I knew he would stay there until the image was burned, until he saw it destroyed and could go home in peace.

"I'm glad you put your arm around Tong tonight," I said quietly. "I wanted to, but it might have looked a little strange."

He squeezed my hand in reply and was asleep.

I lay in the darkness, listening to the gongs and feeling a sense of coming undone, of moving closer to whatever was this magnetic force, this fascinating power without a name. And without knowing when, I crossed over the borders from waking to dreaming, to a place where I knew what it was, yet knew that when I awakened I would not be able to name it.

jumping fish

The intense days of summer flowed into the beginning of autumn, and the children spent days at the beach, enjoying the last of the water before school began. Gordon and I often went with them, and all of us began to turn from pale-skinned Westerners to a shade hardly distinguishable from the dwellers of the village. I sat on the beach, watching Gordon play with the children in the water, watching the older children dive from his shoulders, and little Chris make his first attempts at swimming. In the water there was an unspoken comradeship between all the children, village and ours. Our children could play for hours with someone and never know his name or where he lived. A meeting on the sand or in the water only needed a kind of eye-to-eye relationship that asked nothing more than two live participants and a little sun.

We walked through the market one day on the way home from the beach, sticky with salt and itchy with sand. The street near the Store was crowded with boat people selling fish. It was easy to tell the boat people from the land dwellers by their appearance. Long days on the water had given the fisher people dark brown skin. Their eyes were curiously shiny, and their legs slightly bowed. Whether from diet or balancing on the boats, as some believed, their gait had a peculiar waddle. They sat on the sides of the street, squatted over pails and pans of fresh-caught seafood, calling out their wares in raucous voices.

But on this day, one old woman was different. She sat a bit apart from the rest. She was dressed completely in black, with a rattan fishing hat on, and doubly protected from the sun by a black umbrella over her head. A crowd of shoppers gathered around her, and we listened to what she had to sell, but there was no sound coming from under the umbrella. Curious as to what this extremely soft-sell technique was, I pushed through the crowd to see. There she sat with a metal tub of live fish between her feet, poking them with a small stick. As she poked, the fish jumped up and flopped back into the tub with a silver splash.

"Wah, those are lively!" said a man, and he bought a large one, put it in a plastic bag full of water, and walked away looking pleased with himself.

I watched the old woman's face, brown and wizened in the sun of many summers on the sea. There was a kind of cunning there, a knowing, as she silently poked the fish and made them jump and did a flourishing business.

I went on toward the house, curiously stirred by this sight. The instinctive knowledge that deadness was to be avoided, that only living things carried life and passed it on. What did it say?

China Pearl had mentioned this the day we chopped vegetables and cooked noodles for the crowd.

"We prefer live fish because we believe they still have the life substance in them," she said. "We don't like to eat dead or frozen fish."

"Then what about all the fish laid out on the beach to dry and those big salted fish that hang in the market?" I asked.

She had sighed, a sigh deep for her age, and said that one must eat, and live things were not always available, that sometimes it was a matter of necessity or convenience to take what was on hand.

On the wine factory street, a tiny barber stall was set up. The man clipping hair for students getting ready to return to school looked familiar, yet I could not remember who he was.

"Who's that?" I asked Gordon, who always knew everybody.

"You know, that's Mr. Fong, Ah Wai's husband. We met him at the festival that night."

I had not recognized him. He looked different here on the street, caged in his green stall, snipping hair with his simple tools.

I gave the towels and wet suits to Ah Wai, half-glad and half-guilty that I did not have to contend with the mess myself.

"I saw your *jungfu* on the street," I said. "How's his barber business doing?"

She took a deep breath and dumped the towels in the bathtub.

"Ah, whatever he makes he'll have gambled away before the week is over," she said wearily. "I almost prefer he doesn't work. At least then he's not tempted to gamble. This way he gambles away money before he makes it, and I have to pay off his debts out of my wages."

"Where does he gamble?"

"Ah yah, there are more places than I care to think of. The mahjongg games in the noodle restaurant . . . the big shed next door here, where they listen to the dog races from Macau over the radio and lose everything they have in one night. Does Ding Sang gamble?" she asked suddenly.

"No," I said, laughing. "If we have ten cents we buy a piece of fruit. With four children, who can gamble?"

"Ah yah," she said with that peculiar combination of despair and dreaming. "You and Ding Sang are blessed of heaven. Do you know how lucky you are? Ah yah, here you have been married over ten years, and he treats you like a new bride. You are lucky to care about each other."

I felt she was trying to tell me something.

"Are you and your husband happy?" I asked.

"Ah, you don't understand my way of life. Things have been so different for me. How did you first see your husband?"

"We were introduced by an aunt, and I fell in love the first time our eyes met."

"Ah, as soon as you see, love . . . you have that in your country too? But it always happens to impossible lovers, to people who are somehow prevented from getting married. My life has been so different." She paused, turning on the faucet with a swish. "I was born in Canton, and in those days, forty years ago, a common woman's life was not worth as much as a dog's. If you killed a man's dog, he could bring you to court for it, but if someone beat a woman to death, people looked the other way and said nothing. It was considered a household matter."

"How horrible!"

"Luckily, when I was born, my mother wanted me. She had no other children, and she loved me so much she gave me the name Love . . . I remember I told you that. But when I was seventeen, my father said I was getting too old for him to feed, and a marriage was arranged for me."

"Did you know the man?"

"I never saw him until the day of the wedding. He was ten years older than me and a stranger, and I was frightened. After the first few nights with him, I ran away and tried to come back to my mother's house. But she cried and pushed me out and said I was now the property of the other family, that they had bought me.

"So I went back to live with them, as I had nowhere else to go. I bore two sons and tried to be a good wife to him, and gradually we began to get along well . . . no sweet romantic love, but a kind of getting along."

"Why did he come to Hong Kong before you did?" I asked, remembering the previous conversation.

"Ah," she said, "when the *Kai Fong* liberation government came to China, we had to work very hard. He's never liked work too well, so he decided to run to Hong Kong, try to get an easier way to earn money, and then, perhaps, send for us someday."

"How did you feel about being left alone?"

"Me? I was actually glad the day he left. I still had my two sons, and never caring that much for him, I didn't care when he left. I began to enjoy life. The farmers' group where we lived had organized a people's medical service, and they chose me to be trained as a midwife. I began to learn to read and write and to have a skill. For the first time in my life, I felt important. When the mothers in the village called me and I helped a new life into the world, I felt so happy, like I was doing the most important thing I had ever done." Her eyes were more dreamy than despairing now. "I could have stayed there forever. Even now if he starts acting up, I threaten to go back."

"Then why did you leave?"

"They called me to come here. My husband had found a job, but he gambled away all his money. He had no place to live, nothing to eat, and became so sick he was in the government hospital at the edge of death. They wanted me to come and take care of him."

"How did you feel about that?"

"Feel? How could I feel? He was my husband. If he needed me, I must come. So I came and found him, got a job in a button factory, and nursed him back to health. In the next few years I bore him two more children, a boy and a girl, and now we are poorer than ever—rich in sons, but poor in everything else. Ah yah, he tries, but money never stays in his hands more than a day."

"Did you ever think of divorcing him?" I asked.

"No," she said, smiling her sheepish smile. "That isn't our way. One does what one must, and relationships between people are deeper than always being happy. You're lucky, happiness has come your way. Unhappiness has come to me, and what can be done?"

Jagged pieces of a puzzle were those September days, always listening for the words beyond what was said, the sight beyond what was seen, the Something Bigger.

Gordon was preparing the fall schedule, hiring the last few teachers, and setting up the maintenance staff at school. The older children were making trips on the bus to check about school uniforms at the American School where they would study. Christopher and I were often the only ones left at home, and I found myself building a deep rapport with this small one. I often carried him piggyback or on one hip as I walked through the market streets to protect him from the traffic and the rubble underfoot.

One day he struggled to get down and insisted on walking.

"I'm big now," he asserted. "Why do you hold me so tight?"

"Because if one of those trucks bumped you, you'd get hurt."

"And what would happen to me if I got hurt?"

"We'd have to take you to the hospital and get you fixed."

"And what would happen if the doctor couldn't fix me?"

"Well, then you'd be all broken, and your life would come out of you."

"You mean I'd be dead," he said bluntly.

"I guess so," I said grudgingly.

"And then what?" he said curiously.

"And then I guess you'd go to heaven."

"No, it's not like that, I know, I know. The little piece of God inside me would come out and get stuck back together with the big piece of God!"

"Who told you that?" I said, slightly jarred.

"Myself told myself," he said. "Doesn't yourself ever tell yourself things?"

I looked at him, realizing he would be three at the end of the month.

All summer long, our house had been open all hours of the day and late into the night. Teenagers from the village came when they were free and left at odd hours. That had been fine for the summer with its unmeasured flow of time, its sandy days and hot sleepless nights; now the feeling of fall was getting into our minds, the feeling of organization, of tightening up life to cope with heavier responsibilities.

"One thing I can't take," said Gordon, "is to have kids here all hours of the night if I have to be up at six o'clock and ready for a day of work."

"What can we do?" I asked. "We can't just say to Tong and Tommy and China Pearl and all the others, 'Please go home so we can go to bed!' "

"I've been thinking," he said reflectively. "We may be able to solve two problems with one stroke. Have you ever heard Tommy talk about how badly the town needs a youth center?"

"I'd be deaf if I hadn't. It's one of his main gripes."

"Well, why don't we have a youth center here?"

"Here? Here, in this house?"

"Why not? We practically have one anyhow, with all the kids hanging out here. If we called it something, gave it a purpose, we could organize and control it more."

'Yuck. I don't like the sound of those words," I said.

"And *I* don't especially like the disorganization I find when I come home. I never dare to walk through the house in my underwear or give you a kiss because I never know who's *here,* or where they *are.* But aside from that," he said, "I think we could contribute something to the kids' life in the village by giving them a club, a Youth Club that would meet once a week during stated hours."

"Maybe you're right." I conceded. "Goodness knows I could stand some organization too. How will we do it? Who would it be open to? Everybody?"

"No, I think we should have members . . . make it seem like something special with membership cards . . . maybe even small dues."

"Oh heavens, no dues! People will think we're trying to profit by them!"

"Okay, no dues then. But I still think memberships might be good. What's special about belonging if just anyone can wander in?"

"I'm surprised at you! Don't you know that's the root of every snob club in the world? *What's special about belonging if just anyone can come?* Don't you want something *bigger* than that, something everyone *can* come to?"

"If you have room in the house," he smiled, "and would you like our two heroin addict friends next door to feel free to come in and case the place . . . look where the window handles are located, . . . so they could come in some night and rob us? Aren't you going to use your head at all?"

I felt confused, reaching for the Larger Thing, yet afraid of thieves.

"Let's ask the boys what to do about it," I compromised. "They'll know how to handle it."

Tommy and Wing were guarded that night when we asked them. For once, it was difficult to draw them into a discussion.

"Why don't we get a few more young people together," Tommy hedged. "Say, set a day next week and ask about ten of us to come here and discuss the club."

So the next Friday at seven-thirty was set as a time for discussion.

On the day of the meeting, I baked trays of cookies and prepared drinks, torn between enjoying feeling organized and oppressed by knowing I had to prepare food for invited guests.

At seven-thirty that night we were ready. Gordon had notes drawn up as to how the club should be organized, I had food prepared, and the children were safely stashed away upstairs with instructions not to interrupt us. Everything felt very formal.

At eight o'clock, no one had come. We sat and talked, listening to the lulling sound of the sea and wondering where everyone was. I covered and uncovered the cookie plates, and Gordon reshuffled his notes.

At nine o'clock, not a footstep of the crowd going past had paused at our door. At nine-thirty, we decided that Tommy must have given the wrong date and decided to go to bed.

I covered the plates of cookies for the last time, and Gordon put away his notes. Just as we were getting ready to go upstairs, there was a knock on the door.

Tommy stood in the doorway, his dark eyes blinking shyly in the light and looking completely chagrined. He led the way to the living room and sat down.

"What happened?" Gordon asked.

"I'm very sorry, "Tommy began. "But it won't work, and I didn't know how to tell you."

"What won't work, Tommy?"

He shifted uneasily and blushed.

"Ding Sang, you know we like to come to your house. Here we talk about things. We think new thoughts and find you to be a friend."

"Then what's the problem?"

"The problem is, uh, I don't know how to say. But you know, there are many kinds of people in this town: Wing's parents are Buddhist; the Jengs are leaders in the Kai Fong; some of us come from Communist families. Because we are young, we can all get together and enjoy life as people. But our parents, Ding Sang, they are different. If you start an American Club . . . no matter what you call it that's what it will be because that's what you are . . . our parents will be frightened. They won't want us to belong. They'd be afraid you would make something strange out of us. And if you start a club with *in* people and *out* people, can you see what would happen if you left some of us out or didn't give us a membership card? Ah, Ding Sang,—" he covered his eyes, "there are already so many names fighting for our hearts on this street. Don't be one more power. Can't we just come to your house and be friends?"

I had never seen Tommy so serious. His small frame was trembling, and when he raised his head, his usually shiny eyes were full of pain.

Gordon stuck out his big hand, all but engulfing Tommy's small one.

"Friends," he said a bit hoarsely.

And that was the end of the organization.

The next night, everybody was back as usual.

When we had moved to the village, it had been agreed that the children would have a dual exposure, that their home life would be centered in the Chinese village and their education would remain in the American church and school. This way we felt they would keep an understanding alive in both cultures.

The children seemed to take it all in stride, but after living in the isolation of the village for a summer, *I* began to feel a curious uneasiness when I returned to the Western community. I began to see things through different eyes, to observe objectively what I had once taken for granted with the same questioning eyes I used in the village. Over and through all the questioning was a search for things that contained life over against values that seemed rigid and dead.

I sat in the small, well-furnished chapel like a stranger on Sunday morning, listening to the prelude, wondering if anything was going to happen in the next hour. What was real about the practices and rituals we would participate in? Did we, too, have superstitious practices? The beating of ancestral drums? The assignment of magical values to words and objects?

I watched the people bow their heads and ask a distant God to forgive them, and I thought of the people on the hillside by the sea and of how it was less loss of face to ask forgiveness of the gods than to ask each other's pardon.

During the postlude I sat daydreaming of the old woman and the tub full of jumping silver fish, and hungered for life that stirred and evoked in me an answering stir. Watching the people go through the familiar motions, I felt lonely and isolated, and secretly longed for the street with its press of bodies and squawking chickens, its fragrance and stench, its pulsating reality. Why did I have to come to this solemn, antiseptic place to worship God?

I glanced at the cross, hanging dark and heavy above the altar, and the chalice with its symbolic spilled blood, and felt sad and oppressed. Were these not the symbols of death? They must have tremendous significance to have been so powerful through the centuries. Yet how could I deal with symbols of death when I did not yet comprehend life?

One Sunday morning we were eating breakfast. Gordon was sipping his coffee and looking thoughtful.

"How come you never make apple pie any more?" he asked suddenly.

I laughed. Apple pie in Check Wan village seemed like eating strawberries on the moon.

"With chicken and walnuts?" I asked. "Or sweet bean soup?"

"I wouldn't care for that," he said wryly, "what I'd love is a good roast-beef dinner with apple pie—just for once."

I saw my opportunity.

"I'll make a bargain with you," I said. "If you take the kids to church this morning, I'll cook a good Dutch/American Michigan Sunday dinner for you."

"You shouldn't do that. Can't we have it tonight?"

"No, I really don't feel like going anyhow. You take the older kids, and I'll keep Chris. When you get back, we'll have a real Sunday dinner just like your mom used to make."

I gave him a kiss and felt relieved. It would be good to stay home and get my hands in dough. Perhaps I could concentrate on thinking about it all, without having to go through the *motions*. There was something very earthy about making a pie, something mind-freeing, something believable and solid.

They were gone, shined and polished in their Sunday best. I watched the square green Morris Oxford English car disappear slowly down the crowded market street and turned back to the kitchen.

A Sunday dinner. Potatoes, when was the last time we had eaten potatoes? There were none in the house. Apples? We were even out of apples. There was a piece of beef I had intended to cook with garlic, ginger, rice wine, and green peppers, but I could roast it with carrots—except that there were no carrots.

I picked up the market basket and took Chris's hand to go to Lee Sang's vegetable stall. Down the everyday street we walked, the September breeze from the sea sweeping over the village in invigorating gusts. Life was going on as usual here: Chun Tai tended to her babies; Chun Sang was busy hammering; Wong Tai was cleaning a long silver fish; and Mok Tai was chopping off chunks of meat to hang on hooks. Old Lew was drunk as ever, trying to block out the pain in his crippled back, and Lee Tai was bunching up carrots and green onions for her expected afternoon customers.

I searched the street and sniffed the air. The fragrance of noodles mixed with garlic and ginger spread over the street. Children ran about, and chickens squawked noisily over the barks of dogs. Everything on the street seemed alive, and vaguely unclean.

We stopped at Lee Sang's, and he flashed his gold-toothed smile.

"Ah, Ding Tai, I just saw Ding Sang go to the foreigners' worship place. You didn't go?"

"No, I stayed home," I said, almost apologetically. "Do you have a few potatoes for me and some apples?"

"Ah, Ding Tai, you buying potatoes on foreigners' worship day? I thought you *Yeso* followers didn't buy on Sunday."

"Ah, Lee Sang," I grinned. "this is a mixed-up morning. Everything is happening upside down."

It was on the way back down the street that it happened . . . quietly, gently, like an autumn breeze blowing over my mind. I sniffed the smells of the street again, and looked—looked as though I had never seen it before, and inside me there was a hunger, a wanting to know what this power was that had intrigued me and yet eluded me.

Do such things come in a moment, or a few moments, or over several minutes? It is hard to say, for on such occasions time seems to be of no essence. One moment one is a prisoner in a tight small world with walls and bars fighting to get out, and the next moment there are no bars that could ever again imprison the spirit.

It was simple. I was walking with the basket full of food, holding the hand of my small son; I saw other women carrying baskets, holding small children, and suddenly I had new eyes. I was on the inside of life, and all the rhythms of the sea and the wind were my rhythms. I looked straight into the eyes of the women on the street and smiled, and the smile was the passing of a shared life-awareness. My life was no longer only contained in me but flowed into me from the same source from which it flowed into these others. And the preparation of food, the touch of a child, the sharing of a smile was suddenly a significant act of worship.

I glanced into the Chun's carpenter shop and saw it there, all together. The wood shavings, a virile man, small children playing on the floor, a baby on its mother's back, the perpetual prayer sticks being burned.

Chun Tai smiled, and I found myself smiling back with an ease on my face I had never had. The smile stayed, and I smiled at a ragged old man sitting under the banyan tree. I smiled at the street sweeper and at the women pushing the pig carts. The smile seemed to come from inside me and outside of me, to illuminate the whole street with a shining glow until it shone like a holy place. The people, the stones, the craggy trees, the dogs, the crates, the chickens, the sky, and the sea were caught up in a blaze of holiness until I wanted to throw my hands to the sky and shout for joy!

I stepped into the quiet shade of the front door and set the basket down. On impulse I picked up Chris and hugged him tightly, loving the feel of his small-child arms around my neck.

"Hey, Chris, I love you!" I said hugging him happily.

And in that moment, I knew those were the words to the wind-music I had heard on the street . . . *the words that could touch the center of life . . . who is God . . . who is love . . . "in whom we live and move and have our being."*

When Gordon came home with the older children, I could hardly wait to tell him. He shook his head.

"Where do you get these wild ideas?" he asked. "When are we going to eat?"

"But don't you see how important this is? We don't have to go to a church to find this power. It's right here on the street. Just looking into faces is worship." It sounded somehow *paler* telling him about it.

He leaned against the counter, snitching a piece of pie crust.

"Okay," he said. "So if this life-power is everywhere."

"Yeah?"

He was chewing. "Then wouldn't you find it in church too?"

"Pardon?"

"Isn't this same miracle in the faces of people wherever they are? Wouldn't you find it, even in church?"

I hadn't thought that far.

"I guess," I said a bit hesitantly, still thinking of the somber wooden cross hanging over the altar. I still did not identify with its symbolism but I realized it no longer depressed me. The thing I had just discovered was so large it did not need to negate other things to be true. Nothing would ever be dead again because I had touched what it meant to be alive. Perhaps, in time, more understanding would come.

The Moon Festival was only a week away. Up and down the market streets, moon cakes were bought and sold, four in a box and tied with bright ribbons. The bake shop down the shady rice-shop street did a flourishing business, stamping out the neat pastry cakes with a bright yellow egg-yolk moon inside. Some of the best even contained several moons, surrounded by a dark, sweet bean-paste sky.

The Moon Festival was especially in honor of the women and girls, and every household was busy with preparations. There were three days of feasting: one to welcome the moon, one to enjoy the moon, and one to chase the moon. Sticks of sandalwood would be burned, and paper lanterns must be bought for all the children to carry in the night to welcome and rejoice in the moon.

I went one day to the rice shop to replenish my supply and sat down to talk to China Pearl. Her brothers were teasing her, as usual, and she was trying to chase them all up the ladder to their loft and pull the ladder away. Jeng Tai was tearing her hair out and threatening to beat them all to death if they didn't behave—an idle threat, they knew, since her only weapon was her tongue.

"Those boys," China Pearl pouted, her pretty face looking sullen. "they think they can be funny and tease me about boyfriends just because it's Moon Festival."

"Why at Moon Festival?"

"You know about the Chinese belief that the sun is the male power and the moon the female?"

"Yes, but why are they teasing you?"

"They say I'm getting old and ugly, and I'd better hurry and find a husband this moon festival, or no one will want me."

I looked at her and laughed. Seventeen and far from old and ugly.

"They have this horrible nickname they give me," she explained. "My name, China Pearl, if you don't see the character when it's written, the sound is exactly like Chinese Pig. So whenever I do something they don't like, they call me the Chinese Pig."

It was a relief to know that even placid-looking Chinese brothers and sisters quarreled, and their mothers became distracted.

"What is the Moon Festival about?" I asked her. I had heard various versions but wondered how she would explain it.

She tossed her long hair back and poured a cup of tea out of the ever-ready green thermos and set it in front of me.

"Have you seen the paper lanterns made like rabbits?" she asked. "Those are supposed to represent the rabbit on the moon. He makes medicine by pounding on the root of a cassia tree in a bowl on top of the head of a three-legged toad."

"What's the three-legged toad?" I asked, getting deep into the fantasy.

"The three-legged toad was once a beautiful concubine, the favorite woman of an Emperor. This Emperor didn't want to get old and unable to have sons and die, so he had a pill made for himself, and if he swallowed this pill, he could live forever. He gave this pill to the concubine Heng O to keep safe on her person because she was the only person he trusted. But of course, having this pill, *she* began to worry about getting old and ugly and someday dying, so she decided to swallow secretly the pill so *she* would live forever. But the moment she swallowed it, she became very light and floated up into the sky. She floated up and up until she reached the moon, and there she was turned into an ugly three-legged toad as punishment for her swallowing the pill. That is the toad that holds the bowl while the rabbit grinds the cassia tree into powder."

"So you have a woman on the moon! I laughed. "We always talk about the man in the moon!"

"Oh, there is an old man there too. He arranges marriages and ties spirits together with a long silken cord. It is said that once he binds two spirits together, neither heaven nor earth can keep them apart."

"Has he tied you to anyone yet?"

"I don't know," she said, looking around the rice shop to see if Jeng Tai could hear her. "Sometimes I don't want to marry as young as my mother did. She can't read or write. All she's ever done is have seven children. I might like to leave home and get a job downtown, meet some different people. I want to know more before I settle down."

The market street was in a merry mood on the first day of the festival. Friends invited each other for dinner and carried boxes of moon cakes as gifts. Every business gave moon cakes to its steady customers. Children waved paper lanterns, anxious for the darkness to come so they could light them and frolic on the beach in their bare feet.

Wong Tai came to our door with a box of moon cakes and a cheery smile.

"Come to our house on the mountain, Ding Tai," she said happily. "Tomorrow night, come up and enjoy the moon with us! From the hillside you can see the full moon reflecting over the sea. Ayie, it's a beautiful sight!"

When Gordon came home, I told him about Wong Tai's invitation.

"Did you forget something?" he asked.

"Forget what?"

"The date."

"What date?" I said still looking puzzled.

He looked hurt, and I went to look at the calendar. Tomorrow was his birthday, a day when the two of us always went out together, as we did for mine. It was one of our inviolable dates, like our engagement or wedding anniversary.

"Oh, Gordon, I just didn't think. But why don't we go on up to the Wongs and celebrate with everyone? I think that would be a super way to celebrate this year."

He was quiet, thinking it over.

"It's more involved than that," he said, "we have certain days that are meaningful to us as a couple, as a family; when the choice comes between honoring days that have special significance to us or being drawn into invitations from others, which counts most? I think that's the choice we have to make."

I thought of the kind things he did, and of how important the keeping of small remembrances was, from a first-date anniversary to the single rose he brought home once a week to put in the amber vase in our white room.

And I thought of the gaiety that would take place on the hillside that night, with the moon shining over the sea and the lanterns dancing in the darkness.

"It's up to you," I said.

"No, it's up to you. If it were your birthday, I would insist, but . . ."

We sent Wong Tai our apologies.

But when the darkness came, our children joined the village children with their lanterns lighted for the night of welcome. Up the street and across the beach went the processional of fragile paper lanterns, each lighted by a candle, carried in the wind, precarious, flickering, dangerous and beautiful, while the moon rose over the sea smiling, with her rabbit beating out medicine on the head of the three-legged toad that was once a beautiful concubine.

It was impossible to find a baby-sitter the next night as everyone in the village was deep in the celebration of the Moon Festival. We left the children alone and warned them not to go out of the house. They were angry because they wanted to go to the Wongs, and remembering the trauma that caused last time, we hesitated to let them go.

We went to an expensive restaurant downtown and ordered a steak. It tasted curiously flat.

"Let's stay home next time," Gordon said. He was feeling guilty because it was his birthday that stood in the way. It was so quiet at our table we could hear each other chew. It was the first time in almost fifteen years we had sat in a restaurant feeling like married people who have nothing to say to each other. He felt nervous to say anything because everything he said made him sound selfish, and I felt nervous about replying because everything I said to assure him sounded patronizing.

Finally we gave up and went home without dessert.

And in my mind the puzzle of putting it all together was pounding like the sea . . . that morning I had discovered the oneness of all people, it seemed all the problems of life had been solved. Now I knew they had not, that realizing one's oneness was only the beginning; belonging to everyone was a kind of problem in itself that needed to be solved in careful prioritizing, like this night. How much of me belonged to all the people around me and how much to special people?

When everyone returned from school, I became the listener. Each day Marita, Michael, and Deidra returned from school on the bus and made their way down the market street in the blue uniforms of the

American School. One day Mike stormed in the door and threw his books on the table.

"What is it, Mike?"

"They've taken the grades off learning Chinese in school," he said. "I mean, it doesn't count for the Honor Roll any more. Lots of the kids are going to take French instead because their parents think it's better for their future. I wanted to learn more Chinese, but the kids don't listen to the teacher, and there's not much order in the class. They even call her a Dumb Chink . . . and she's a *nice* lady."

He looked at me with troubled eyes, and all I could do was give him a hug.

Later, Gordon came home, tired from a day of working in the Chinese school, frustrated with the nuances of his situation. Biblical Knowledge was a required subject in the British school system as a part of Western culture, and as Gordon was the foreigner, Bible and English became his natural inheritance in the teaching slots. Separately, they both had creative possibilities and were interesting to present to the students, but the connections that sometimes grew in the students' minds were startling.

There was the student who had written across his Biblical Knowledge test paper,

"Please excuse my English. I do believe in God."

Sometimes it was painful to see the pointed stabs people made at reaching across the barriers, the ways in which they avoided feeling the responsibility of relating directly to the lives of one another.

In the American community, all the students were out of school for the Western festival of the harvest, Thanksgiving. On Thanksgiving Day, a large truck pulled into the streets of Check Wan village. Two American men jumped out of the truck and began taking out boxes of canned goods, flour, sugar, and other groceries, distributing them to the "poor" of the village.

Mrs. Wong, Mrs. Yau, the Lees, the Moks, and the Jengs stood open-mouthed as boxes of goods were deposited in front of their shops with the foreign words, "Happy Thanksgiving."

Some of the food was fed to the pigs, some poured out, and some selected things kept. Most of it was inedible, from the villagers' point of view. They thought the foreign men had gone crazy and had no idea that their deed had stemmed from good and even religious intentions.

But the next Sunday when I went to the chapel, I heard people expressing thanks that the foreigners had had opportunity to share with those less fortunate than they.

. . . and I looked around at the faces, wondering who was fortunate and who was unfortunate, and thinking of the ways we all use symbols to exorcise the ghosts of misunderstanding and prejudice, and pondering the fears that snobbery perpetuates.

Tommy was worried. In a few months he must take an examination in English, and on the strength of passing that test, he would be eligible for a promotion in a downtown bank. His mother needed the money to raise the other children, and Tommy was terrified of failure, of letting her down.

"She's taken care of me all these years. I should at least help her now," he said.

Gordon offered to help Tommy improve his grasp of written English.

"Keep a small notebook full of things you think are important each day," Gordon instructed him. "And at night I'll look over your English and help you with sentence formation, punctuation, and spelling."

Tommy grasped eagerly at the chance.

One night when I was upstairs reading the nightly story to the children, I heard them talking quietly on the couch. When Gordon came up, I asked him what the discussion was about. He smiled a tender, amused smile.

"Tommy wants to know how you can tell when you're in love," he said.

"And what did this wise, experienced old man say?"

"I just let him talk first. I guess the night of the Moon Festival he was invited over to the Jengs, and somehow he and China Pearl ended up sitting on the beach behind their house. They talked and at one point he reached out and took her hand. He said just touching her hand was the most exciting thing he had ever done in his life . . . it was as though it pulled him out of himself, and he wanted to go on holding her hand forever."

"Did he kiss her?"

I don't think so. The way he talked about that hand, kissing was unnecessary. These kids are so shy and beautiful and gentle."

"I know. Do you hope our kids can grow up here?"

"I don't know," he said. "Would it be right for them?"

"People aren't that different," I said. "I remember the first night you held my hand."

"So do I," he said softly. "So do I."

In the middle of the night I heard Chris stir in his sleep. I jumped up and went down the stairs to see about him, but when I reached his bed he was fast asleep, mumbling baby words in a dream.

I covered him and went back up the stairs. Halfway up the stairway there was a small window, oddly placed, that looked more like a round peep-hole than a window. I glanced outside and saw a strange sight. In the shed halfway up the hill, the drug addicts had built a small fire. In the total darkness of the night the fire glowed orange and eerie, with the shadowy shapes of the men crouched over it.

Far away down the street, I could hear the clatter of the all-night game of mah-jongg going on in the noodle shop, and I knew that the men of the village were there, gambling away the money that was needed for school fees, for food and clothing, and I knew that in the night the shrill voices of wives would be heard, calling for the men to come home.

I thought of the day when I knew this street to be a holy place, the day when every person seemed illumined with a glow and all existence seemed hallowed; it seemed incongruous with the sounds of the night.

And then I watched the men crouched over their fire and wondered why I had ever expected that on a holy street there would be no pain, no struggle, no hurt.

I went up the stairs thinking of the old woman and her jumping fish, of the hunger in the stomachs of people to eat life, and how sometimes it was a matter of necessity or survival to settle for slightly less.

light a red candle

In a world of ghosts and devils, pig herders and floating concubines, angels, shepherds, and virgins seemed far removed. Even Santa Claus, who had no snow for his sleigh nor chimneys to descend, seemed oddly out of place.

But it was December. Christmas was coming. Christmas, with the smell of salt and sea and rice wine on the morning fog instead of sugar and spice and all things white and nice.

Of all the years we had spent in Hong Kong, this was the first time we would actually spend a Christmas living in the village. With a dreadful feeling that it might be the last one spent there, I wanted deeply to celebrate it in a way to be remembered forever. Yet we were both aware that it was a foreign holiday, not to be pushed on our neighbors or taken for granted that they even wanted to celebrate it.

Tommy and Tong came over one evening early in December.

"We've shared our festivals with you," Tommy said. "Now it's your turn to tell us what the Western festival of Christmas means."

"Did they teach you about Christmas in the Western school?" I asked.

"They taught us about the baby god who got born on Christmas, the heavenly messengers, and the scholars riding on camels."

I looked at Tong and knew this explanation did not satisfy him.

"It's also a celebration of peace," I said. "Of peace and giving, of sharing what is yours to keep. It's a time when people feel one with each other."

But Tong looked at me as though these too were hollow words.

"You can't tell what a festival is about," he insisted. "They always sound strange and empty when one tries to tell. A festival has to be *experienced,* has to be *felt.*"

"With the gongs beating?" I asked, remembering.

"With the gongs beating," he agreed, a smile on his smooth face.

In the beginning, the gongs seemed all wrong. It was still hot. There was a long, stagnant war being waged in Vietnam, no Christmas trees for sale, and life was going on as usual. There was no excitement in the air because no one on the market street cared if it were soon to be Christmas. The convent school on the edge of town had put up a wooden creche, and the toy shops in the village laid out a few plastic blow-up Santas, but they seemed foreign and forlorn in the swarming village streets. The day could have come and gone with no one missing it.

Then we remembered the red candle.

The window overlooking the street was a perfect place for a candle, a red candle of welcome and celebration and joy. It had to be a *thick* red candle, carved with a happiness character that would stand out when it was lit, a symbol that expressed happiness not only to us in the house but to everyone who passed on the street. When we moved into this house, we had decided to light a red candle in the window at Christmas.

So Gordon bought a brass niche to shield it from the wind, and we found the right red candle, thick and sturdy and carved with double happiness to set up over the street.

Ah wai came to work and saw the candle.

"Christmas," she said. "My son will be a wise man in the play at the school, and I'll go to watch him."

I was surprised, after her talk about China.

"Are you a follower of the Yeso teaching?" I asked.

"No, I'm a member of the Heaven-Lord Church, where the God-Father says mass. My son was lucky to get into their school. It's hard to find a place I can afford to send my children. They're doing a good thing for my son, so why not join them? Ah yah, names mean nothing to me. I say when in China, do what you must and when in Hong Kong, be whatever is convenient. Ah yah, be whatever you must, I say, just so you're a good person and your children can eat."

I watched her sweep the floor, and looked at her life-weary face, and understood.

"What size sweaters do your children wear?" I asked, wanting to change the subject. "I'd like to get them something warm for when the weather changes."

"Ayie, Missy, don't buy my children anything, please. I can't buy anything for yours and I would be embarrassed. Please, no gifts."

I looked at her again and knew that celebrating Christmas in the village would need to be done with care. Even sharing what we had would not bring peace if it were not done gently, and with understanding.

Gordon and I sat sipping our coffee one morning, wondering what to do.

"Were we going to buy something small for the village kids who come here regularly?" I asked. "Kids like Tommy and Wing and China Pearl?"

"Where would you stop?" he said. "I think we'd get into trouble doing that. God knows we're not all that affluent, but giving things *en masse* always creates that impression. Handouts depersonalize people."

I looked up at the window, at the brass niche with the red happiness candle, and a feeling came over me like the morning I was standing on the balcony, a little breath of the wind-song from the street, a song without words, but a deep wistfulness.

"How about a party?" I said, following the wistful feeling with no idea where it was going.

He set his cup down suddenly and looked at me.

"A village party?"

"A village party—for *everybody!*"

I saw his eyes light up. "You could bake all sorts of Christmas cookies, and I could buy some tapes of Christmas music."

"Not too religious," I said. "We don't want to scare them."

"No, I won't, but we *could* invite everybody!"

"We *could!* That's a great idea! Everybody! Gordon, it's going to be Christmas on this street! It's going to be wonderful! Can't you feel it?"

I stopped, afraid I was going to disgrace myself by crying in my coffee. I glanced at him and saw his face soften too, and I knew the candle was getting to us, sitting there waiting for us to catch up.

Tommy came to help us write up the list of invitations. We listed Wong, Mok, Lew, Yau, Jeng—all the names whose faces were familiar. But there was the dread of leaving someone out, especially at Christmas, a time when everyone should be included.

"That's no problem, if it really worries you," Tommy explained. "You see, everyone in this village is related either by blood or by marriage. Name all the people you know, to make it personal, and write the invitations *Tung Ga,* with family, so any relative of these people can feel welcome. That way no one will lose face."

So the invitations were written Tung Ga on red shiny folders with Tommy's careful black ink characters drawn in polite form.

We began to scurry around getting ready for the big party. The grey cement courtyard was painted green to extend the living room, and with the red brick wall and the many plants that had now been contributed by friends in the village, it could almost be called a garden patio. The children and I made endless trips through the market to the Store to buy supplies of flour, sugar, nuts, dried fruits, and other ingredients for Christmas treats. There were already fruit cakes mellowing upstairs in a box under the bed, and every day new containers of traditional treats joined them. The refrigerator was stacked high with airtight boxes to keep the crispier goodies fresh.

I began to feel as though the magic of Christmas could overcome anything, as though it could bind together the deep dark wounds of the world, and the walls built between persons.

When I went to the Store, I smiled at Hong Sang, and he looked at me with a kind of astonishment. He picked up the packages of ingredients as though they were imported poisons, wrote down the price, and dismissed my smile with a curt nod. But I was too full of the Christmas feeling, too full of red candlelight to be discouraged.

"You must come to the party, Hong Sang," I invited him doubly, "and see what we make out of all your ingredients."

"Yes, thank you," he nodded, with a no-thank-you-please look on his face. I went out the door and down the steps, thinking it would be much more pleasant to celebrate Christmas in the village if Hong Sang were not in the Store guarding our nuts and raisins like a grouchy old dragon.

One day Gordon was with me at the Store when I repeated the invitation.

"We'll be expecting you!" I said cheerily, as we went out the door.

Gordon poked me when we were safely outside.

"Why do you keep saying that?" he asked. "Don't you know he'd get laughed out of town if he came? Can't you see that? Leading Communist in Chek Wan village comes to American Christmas party? Who do you think you're kidding?"

"Well, he might just come. You never can tell."

"I'll bet he won't," Gordon insisted.

The gambling spirit of the street was rubbing off on me.

"I'll bet he will," I said stubbornly.

"How much you bet?"

"Five bucks, stolen out of your back pocket!"

"Ah yah!" he yelped, clutching at his billfold pocket, and I realized how Chinese we were getting, even at Christmas.

The Jeng boys and Tong had promised to get us a tree. Since the party was set for the fifteenth, and there would be no trees for sale in Hong Kong by that time, their plan was to wait until the policemen were occupied on the other end of town and then go up the hillside to cut a small tree. It was not legal, but not *illegal,* they argued, because the land belonged to no one except the government, and since it belonged to no one, cutting a tree for a party for *everyone* was not stealing. I wasn't too sure about this logic but decided to go along with it, since it seemed to be the only way to get a Christmas tree.

But day after day I waited for the tree. Every time I asked Gordon and he asked the boys, they said the policemen were sitting in this end of town, and they could not get one yet.

"What if the day comes for the party and we don't have a tree?" I asked.

"We will," Gordon promised.

"You say we will," I said. "But that won't make it happen. What if the day comes and we don't *have* a tree?"

"Then, the worst thing that could happen is we won't."

"But we can't have a Christmas party without a tree!"

"We could."

"Well I couldn't! I want you to get after those boys if they're going to get one and tell them to get moving!"

"Now who's getting formal and uptight?"

"This is different," I said. "It's Christmas, and things have to be a certain way."

"I didn't know you still had a traditional bone in your body," he said.

"But this is *different*," I insisted. "We're trying to show someone else what our festival is like, and we have to be authentic, do it right."

"But isn't it the spirit that counts?"

The children were out of school for Christmas vacation and beginning to get excited. It was still warm and sticky outside, but no one in the village went swimming anymore. Only foreigners and tourists and the old European up on the hill could be seen at the beach, and in the absence of other children, our children stopped going.

The front steps were more crowded than ever, but now it seemed normal, a sound without which one would notice the stillness. When I baked, I took warm sugar cookies out for the step sitters to sample, and while the door was open, three or four would wander in to play with Chris, or Tommy's sister Suk Jing would come to play dolls with Deidra. Ah Wai sometimes brought her youngest son of seven, and he entertained Chris with small games and drawings. The sea washed lazily up on the beach, the wind brushed softly over the streets, and I began to believe that it was true there could be peace on earth and goodwill was a simple gesture within the reach of my hands.

Then one day the mail came, a swish and a plop under the front door, and I went to get it.

Cards from what used to be home—from friends and family. Cards with chubby blond angels and hallowed Madonnas, with laughing fat Santas and solemn verses, all statements that would sound as strange to the people on this street as Tommy's description of the Devil Festival had sounded to us. But I looked again at the chunky red candle in the window, something East and West, warm and bright, and felt that with care, worlds could meet.

Then I picked up the magazine that came in the mail and stood in the hallway leafing through it. I looked, and looked again, my heart slowly began to pound. The war in the country of the South Moon: *Yeut Naam.* Something had gone wrong. War was terrible, but now even the brutal rules of war were being violated. *Photographs of young American soldiers standing over the bodies of Asian women and children who looked like the market people—children—oh my God—the children looked like the little flock of birds sitting on the front steps.*

I stared at the red of the blood and the green uniforms, realizing numbly that they were the colors of Christmas. Then I covered my face and began to cry.

The next time I walked through the market, my eyes were down. *Peace on earth.* I felt ashamed of the red invitations we had given out in the village. I bought vegetables from Lee Sang, saw the crackling transistor radio perched on the ginger roots, and knew he knew. At the Jeng's rice shop, I could tell they knew but were too polite to say anything. Everyone *knew,* but it was too heavy a thing to talk about. Only Lee Sang spoke of it gently, with his gold teeth gleaming.

"Don't carry it in your heart, Ding Tai," he said kindly. "In every country there are the good and the evil, and all men have a little evil in them. Don't carry it on your shoulder. People understand."

I hoped he was right.

But when I went to the Store, Hong Sang no longer nodded curtly. He nodded smugly, watching me like a cunning cat, wondering at the foolish combination of savagery and conscience my kind displayed. I said no more to him about the party and silently hoped he would forget it.

The fifteenth was a giant seesaw of hope and fear, sureness and bittersweet disaster.

That morning the tree had not come, and Gordon had gone downtown to see if there might be an early arrival in some other section of the city.

The children excitedly raced up and down the green terrazzo stairs after each other, and I was sure someone would have a broken bone by night. It had been months since we had given or gone to a party, and this, in addition to Christmas coming, had them in high gear.

It was Ah Wai's day off, but she had polished and shined the house the day before, ready for Wong Tai's scrutiny. I slipped the lock on the front door so the stream of traffic would be temporarily stopped and latched the orange door in the courtyard. By the time the night was over, the place would be a mass of footprints, but I at least wanted to start out clean.

The bulk of the baking was done, but there were a few more stars and angels and Santas I wanted to cut out and decorate.

Mike came into the kitchen.

"Mom, do you remember you said we could make a gingerbread house for the party tonight, you know, the one you always make?"

I started to turn and tell him to run out and play, to leave me alone. Then I remembered that getting all impatient with my own children to put on a splendid Christmas display for the village was not the thing to do.

I hesitated, softening.

"Do you think you can do it without making too much mess? The party's tonight, you know."

"I know. I'd like to help if I could."

What mother could resist that offer from a shaggy eleven-year-old on the verge of growing up when such things would not be heard?

I got out the pattern, sugary and stiff from years of making gingerbread houses, began mixing the spicy molasses dough, and set him up as official gingerbread man. In a few minutes the girls were in the kitchen too, and little Chris was on a stool, up to his elbows in the wonderful softness of the flour can, looking more like a snowman than anything I'd seen for years. Even his eyelashes were powdered.

I looked at them and recaptured the warm feeling of being together here in this tiny whitewashed kitchen even if the world outside were falling apart. I watched Mike's sturdy hands, cutting out the cookie-house pattern, and tried not to think of the fact that he was only seven years younger than some of the soldiers in the pictures—*that in seven years those innocent hands would be old enough to kill.*

We laid out the baked pieces to cool, mixed the icing, and tried to keep from eating all the colored candies before they went on the roof.

Mike was impatient.

"Can we put it all together now, Mom? Can I?"

"Wait a while, Mike, I think it's too soft yet."

"Okay," he agreed.

I turned to watch the girls' star points and angel wings, and the next thing I knew Mike exclaimed. He had put the roof on the sides, and the whole house had collapsed.

That must have been the point at which I decided the children had done their share, and I could manage better without them.

It was noon by the time the children were washed up, and I was beginning to feel tense about the party. There was still no tree. What if the villagers felt unsure about us because of the war and simply did not show up? What if they blamed us personally or by inference as *one of those people* and were too polite or elusive to say so? What if nobody came?

Yet on the other hand, Tommy had written a sizeable pile of invitations, and with his little words Tung Ga, everyone in the village had been invited. The house might be jammed! I suddenly wondered if there would be enough to eat and began compulsively stirring up another batch of brownies.

"Mom, are you nervous or something?" Marita asked.

"Well, you know how it is before a big party," I said.

"Do you want me to take Chris down to the playground for you?" Mike offered.

"Would you?" I said, giving him a hug. "I'd appreciate that!"

"Can we get an ice cream cone on the way back?" he asked.

I reached into the change basket on top of the refrigerator and found a Hong Kong dollar. "Here, take this," I said. "And remember, nothing but ice cream. I do *not* want you getting those orange popsicles all over your face and shirt, because I don't have time to give Chris another bath."

Mike hoisted Chris on his shoulders and headed for the door.

"Okay, Mom," he said.

I glanced at the poor gingerbread house, looking like Poe's fallen house of Usher.

"And don't just say okay!" I called after him. "Remember!"

"Okay," he called back and then stopped, looking chagrined. This *okay* was getting to be a habit with him, perhaps because it was one of the few English words the village children understood. Okay-Miko was his village nickname.

"Oh, Mike," I groaned, and watched him go out the door and into the busy street full of swill carts, dogs, fishermen, chicken crates, and vegetable sellers. He looked small and blond and vulnerable, and I resolved to be patient with him. He was never deliberately disobedient, just absent-minded—absent-minded and generous to a fault. Sometimes

I feared some of the less friendly elements in the village would take advantage of his gentle ways.

He disappeared around the bend beyond the banyan tree, and I began to have the familiar feeling of uneasiness about sending the children to the Store. All up and down the market street I had no fear; Lee Tai or Yau Tai would treat our children as their own. But Hong Sang was a different character. It was as though he was not free to relate to us as persons, as though because of his strong political orientation he could see us only as six examples of imperialist aggression. Perhaps he did wonder if we were spies, under the guise of an innocent family, with even our smallest members gathering information in this Asian village.

I watched the crowd close in behind my sons and sighed. They were too young to understand the sting of prejudice.

At three o'clock I was still wondering what to do if no Christmas tree came when Mike came in the door with Chris on his shoulders. At his heels followed a crowd of small children from the village playground. They spilled into the house behind him calling "Miko, Miko-okay!" and laughing.

I looked at Mike, wondering where Gordon was staying so long, and then I saw the orange stains around Chris' mouth and down the front of his shirt.

The tension and frustration of everything that had and had not happened crept into my voice, giving it a sharp edge.

"Mike, I thought I told you not to buy those filthy orange popsicles! Now why did you do it?"

The laughter suddenly ceased, and Mike looked at me. His mouth opened, and then he glanced at the crowd of children and closed it. One by one they silently sneaked out and left him standing. He took Chris off his shoulders and started upstairs.

"Mike?" I called after him. "Why don't you ever listen to me?"

There was no answer except the vehement slamming of his door.

By four o'clock Gordon was home, and I was glad to see him. There were still a hundred things to do. The Jeng boys had finally managed to get a tree from the hillside and brought it in through the orange courtyard door, away from the street and the eyes of the policemen. Gordon and the boys stuck it in a bucket of beach sand and decorated the branches with pine cones painted bright red, yellow, and blue, a handmade present from the Jeng family. The poor tree looked a bit lopsided, as though it had clung to the hillside for dear life through many typhoons, and I began to feel it was an inappropriate symbol of the occasion.

The last batch of cookies still needed icing, and we were out of powdered sugar. The change basket on top of the refrigerator reminded me of Mike, and I ran upstairs.

He was still in his room, reading a book.

"Mike, what did you start to say to me a while ago?" I asked.

He turned his head to the wall and covered his face with the book he was reading. "Nothing" was all he would say.

It was unlike him and troubled me. He seemed more hurt than angry, and I wanted to ask him what it was all about, but there was no time to talk.

Going down the stairs, I wondered if Hong Sang had been rude to him or cheated him.

It was Ah Wai's day off, but at the last minute she decided to come and help. She had been invited as a guest, but the strain of switching roles was too much for her. I could sense her uneasiness at sitting next to Wong Tai who had recommended her as a servant, letting me do the serving. The thought was too embarrassing.

At five o'clock, just as I was feeding the family, she appeared in a freshly done beauty parlor hairdo and a neat grey sam-fu pajama.

"Missy, I'll help you tonight," she said, with her shy smile.

I wished to goodness, just at Christmas, she'd call me something more human than *Missy*.

"No, Ah Wai, you're my guest tonight."

"No, it would have a bad meaning."

I saw it was one of those matters of respect and useless to fight.

Her husband and three of their four children stood in the doorway behind her.

"They've come to be guests," she said. "I've come to help."

Mr. Fong and the children filed into the living room and sat down. Besides having a helper, I had three guests two-and-a-half hours early.

By six o'clock, the street outside was dark, and much quieter than usual. I heard the pounding of waves on the beach and the howl of a street dog and shivered with excitement. The house was ready. The dining room table was stretched to its limit and crowded with dishes of baked goods: fruit cakes, sugar stars, red-decorated Santas, pink and white angels, chocolate brownies, and in the center, Mike's repaired gingerbread house. As a last minute thought, there was a large salad bowl filled with peanuts for those who might not like the sweets.

In the window that faced the street, the sturdy red candle stood, flickering its welcome in the gathering darkness.

Tommy and Wing had volunteered to pour tea, and with Ah Wai to marshal their resources, soon every pot and pan in the house was filled with boiling water. I had time to get the children ready and tried unsuccessfully to untangle the problem with Mike, while Gordon made conversation with Fong Sang in the living room. I noticed him talking steadily to Gordon and wondered how life sounded from *his* perspective. I could imagine his story of his brave escape from the Mainland, of the difficulties of life in Hong Kong, and jokes about this unmanageable woman he was married to.

At seven o'clock, just when the first guests should be arriving, the telephone rang. I jumped, wondering who was dialing to say they could not come.

But the voice at the other end of the line was an American, a voice from last year's world.

"I don't know how you and Gordon feel about the recent developments in Vietnam," she said, "but you seem like the kind of people who would be concerned. We're getting a group together tonight to plan a demonstration in front of the American Consulate tomorrow, and we thought you might like to join us."

The voice sounded unreal, like some official way to handle tears, something I did not want to think of on this night of celebration.

"I'm sorry, we've got a party tonight."

"Couldn't you break it off for something this important?"

"Not really. We're not attending, we're giving a party. We've got the whole village coming in a few minutes. Look, can I call you back? They should be arriving any minute."

"Oh, I'm sorry. How about tomorrow? Shall we sign you up for tomorrow?"

"I don't know. I'll see. I'll get back to you."

I hung up, feeling strange in the pit of my stomach, the same dreaded feeling coming back that had gripped me that afternoon. How did we know anyone would come under the circumstances? After all, we were from the "other side."

At seven-thirty, no one had arrived. The three children who were tall enough were snitching peanuts out of the wooden bowl.

"No one's going to come," I said desperately.

"Relax," Gordon reminded me, "remember in Chinese, it's seven o'clock until it's eight. Anyhow, the Fongs are here, and Tommy and Wing. That's enough to have a party."

There was a timid knock on the door. Gordon opened it, and Tommy's younger sister Suk Jing came in, a bright pink ribbon from the moon cake boxes in her hair. She was carrying a packet of oranges. Behind her came a procession of teenaged girls, then boys, then adults, grandparents, babies, people from the meat stall, the vegetable stalls, the fish stall: the Chuns, the Wongs, the Moks, the Lews, the Lees, and the Yaus.

We stood at the doorway greeting each one, smiling and saying more in relief than in courtesy, "Oh *thank* you for coming! You give us great face by coming to our house tonight!"

The crowd in the living room jostled and drank tea, elbow to elbow. The children tasted the cookies and dropped them on the floor as too sweet, and ate handfuls of peanuts instead. Mok Tai, the elegantly thin lady from the meat stall, also declined the sweets.

"Ah yah, so beautiful," she sighed. "I would like to eat it, but those sweet things give me hot airs."

I glanced at the table, thinking in despair of the hours and dollars I had spent baking. Tomorrow the whole village would be sold out of Chrysanthemum tea, drunk to counteract the *hit hey,* hot airs, caused by the sweets. I felt a stab of resentment until I remembered the Moon Festival and the difficulty Gordon and I had choking down moon cakes, even those pronounced the finest.

Somewhere in the crowd I met Gordon. He was on his way upstairs to get the tape recorder.

"Have you seen your friend Hong Sang?" he asked.

"No! Is he here?"

"No. Did you expect him?"

I saw that he was teasing. I dashed off to fill a teapot, wondering if I really had expected Hong Sang.

Tommy pressed his way through the crowd, furiously pouring tea. The room was a blur of voices. Above the singsong Cantonese conversations, the whir of the recorder rose, projecting a little girl's voice softly singing a Mandarin song. It grew quiet and the children giggled, and one little girl covered her face.

"That's not me!"

"Yes it is! Ding Sang stole your voice in that box!"

The laughter, the crowd. It was warming up, physically warming up with the press of bodies. I could feel something beginning to happen, a current running around the room. I wanted to move through the crowd, to touch everyone, to make anything right that was wrong or hurt. My eyes met Wong Tai's, and I remembered the invitation to watch the moon come up over the sea from her house. Had she been as hurt as I would have been if no one had come tonight?

I went to where she was, squatting against the wall near the little Christmas tree as she did in the market, looking as relaxed and self-possessed as a cat. I sat on the floor beside her and sipped tea with her, my tea this time.

"I hope you understand why I didn't come up to your house the night of the Moon Festival," I said.

She nodded.

"To keep peace at home is the most difficult task," she said. "Wing told me it was Ding Sang's birthday that night."

I smiled gratefully and patted her shoulder, then moved through the crowd.

. . . the buzz of voices . . . looking into faces without the trappings of our daily roles as customer and shopkeeper, foreigner and native . . . I felt the seconds slipping through my fingers and wanted to close my hands and grasp them . . . children's voices, laughing in a game of tag in the courtyard. It was good, a moment precariously suspended in time . . . fragile . . . needing to be savored . . . I wanted it to last forever. . . .

The adults left as suddenly as they had come, in a group saying they must close up the stalls for the night, and took the smaller children with them. There were smiles and vows to do this more often, not to let the whole year pass before we sat together again.

Left on their own, the teenagers had other ideas.

"Do you mind if we dance?" Tommy asked timidly.

We knew that a party was not a real party to Hong Kong teenagers without dancing, so Gordon brought out the tapes he had bought in anticipation of the request, Western style rock tapes of the "Rudolph the Red Nosed Reindeer" type sold downtown in Hong Kong. Soon the living room and the patio were filled with gyrating teens, Chinese faces dancing to Hong-Kong/Western music, representatives of an emerging world, doing the dance of all nations.

At ten o'clock, Tommy remembered the sick man next door and suggested we go inside to be more quiet. As they were coming in the patio door, one of the Jeng boys picked up a harmonica the children had left lying on top of a pile of toys, blew into it, and began to play. In a matter of seconds, several young voices had picked up the melody of "It Came Upon the Midnight Clear" and were singing the Chinese words to the carol.

"On the earth peace, May friendship increase."

Gordon and I looked at each other, as surprised as if the angels had arrived on the patio. We were still staring as every voice in the room picked up the carol, drowning out the thumping recorded music.

Gordon snapped off the tape recorder and began to sing with them, a small, soft smile playing around the corners of his eyes. I could not make a sound.

"Who taught you that?" Gordon asked when the song was done.

"We know all your Christmas songs!" They laughed, clapping and enjoying his amazement. "We've always known the words, but we've never had a foreign friend celebrate your festival with us before!"

Around the living room floor we settled into a circle, the flicker of soft candlelight and the catastrophic mess of squashed stars and headless angels surrounding us. We joined hands and smiled and looked into each other's faces, people from two sides of the world singing the same song.

I saw Tong, sitting cross-legged with his eyes closed and a half-smile on his face, wordlessly swaying to the music.

I wanted to go and sit beside him, to join in his wordless music that was like the wind from the sea, the wind in the banyan tree, but the music in the room had words, my words, inadequate as words always are, but the best I knew . . .

> Peace on earth,
> Goodwill to men
> From Heaven's all gracious king . . .
> The world in solemn stillness lay
> To hear the angels sing.

One by one the children had slipped upstairs to go to sleep, and the young people were just leaving when the phone rang again. It was Hong Sang.

"So sorry I didn't make it tonight," he said apologetically. "I was coming but was held up in a meeting in Central—"

I was shocked, still in the dreamlike euphoria of the party. Why was he apologizing? I really hadn't expected . . .

"Oh yes, Hong Sang, I'm sorry you didn't make it too. We missed you, but I did save some of the treats for you."

"No need to be so polite." His voice over the phone was unusually cordial. "Ding Tai, can you come to the Store in the morning? I have a little something for your family. Or shall I send it by the delivery boy?"

"Oh, no, no. I can come."

I hung up, not sure I had heard him properly. What had changed *him* so much?

I went upstairs to tuck in the children. Mike had fallen asleep with his jeans on. The breeze from the water had turned cooler, and I threw a light blanket over him, still pondering the loose ends of the day.

Gordon and I swept up the debris in the living room and stuffed it into plastic bags to set out under the banyan tree. Then we blew out the candle and stood together in the darkness, breathing in its bittersweet smoke and listening to the pounding of the sea.

"I forgot to tell you," I said. "Somebody called, and asked if we'd like to join an antiwar demonstration tomorrow."

He glanced at his watch by the light from the street lamp outside the window.

"It's already tomorrow," he said. "And I feel demonstrated out, don't you?"

I hurried through the market streets the next morning and up the stone steps to Hong Sang's store, curious yet on guard. Always these unexpected turns of events. Why didn't he simply come or not come? As a token of goodwill, I clutched the lumpy tin foil packet of homemade cookies, rescued from last night's party.

I felt the difference as soon as I walked into the Store. Hong Sang came from behind his counter, almost naked without it. He graciously accepted the packet and then brought out a sumptuous basket of fruit, nuts, and candies with a big bottle of whiskey laid across the top.

"But Hong Sang—"

He interrupted me with a wave of his hand. "Don't mention it. Don't mention it."

"But Hong Sang, I—"

He seemed anxious to tell me something. He squinted slightly behind his thick glasses, his face strained.

"Your eldest son," he was saying. "How old is he?"

"Eleven," I answered. "But why?"

"He will be a good man," he said unblinkingly. "What do you teach him?"

I stared at him, still not comprehending. His face had an open, inviting expression that I had never seen on it before.

"Yesterday," he was saying, "your son came to my store with a dollar to spend. There were eight children from the street who came in with him. Those children did not bring money. He started to use the whole dollar for himself and his brother to have an ice cream cone and then changed his mind and treated everyone to ten-cent popsicles. Tell me, is this what you teach your son?"

I felt it all blurring together—the rush, the frantic trying, the absent-minded Mike, generous to a fault—and I wanted to give a cheer for all the gentle people who have looked beyond the hate and fear and have ironically changed the world by being too giving. I wanted to give a cheer for Yeso himself, but Hong Sang's Store hardly seemed the place.

And then across that dumbfounded astonishment, I saw Hong Sang reaching out his hand. I clasped it and heard him say, "Ding Tai, I believe we have something in common. I wish you and your family Holy-Birth-Festival happiness."

All the floating concubines and pig carts in the world could not have kept the street from looking like Christmas as I struggled back through the market with the big basket. The wind from the sea had turned brisk. People who had been at the party last night smiled and waved. The green Bok Choy and other vegetables at Yau Tai's stall looked like holly and ivy, and the spicy red sausages hanging from their strings at the meat stall could have doubled for Fifth Avenue ornaments. Everything, just as it was, seemed to shout "Joy to the World."

Mike was coming out of the door as I reached it. I set the basket down, put my hands on his shoulders, and looked into his face.

"I found out why you bought the popsicles," I said breathlessly.

He looked at me uncertainly.

"Was it . . . okay?" he asked.

"You're some okay kid," I said hugging him so hard it hurt us both.

There was a sigh of relief from the shaggy blond head nestled under my chin, and I knew that even if the twenty-fifth never came, it had already been a great Christmas.

On Christmas Eve we usually opened our presents, but that year we accepted an invitation from the village teenagers. Marita and Deidra decided not to go, but Mike joined us in the walk through the night. It had turned brisk and, accustomed to months of hot sun, we shivered in the forty-degree weather.

Across town we walked past villas by the swimming beach, down the main bus road to the convent, where a little Chinese nun came out and showered us with homemade candies as though she had waited for us all year, down the steep hill into the market, past the tailor shop and the hardware, singing in Chinese and English. Past the Ma's, who were second in power in the village Communist structure. Past the Jeng's rice shop, where steel bars were drawn for the night. Past the odds and ends shop, where the emaciated little baby lie in her box, a strange manger on this night of serenading Asian angels.

Past the snake-wine shop and the plastic toy shop, where the bloated plastic Santas waved stiffly in the cold wind. Past Yau Tai's, where she peered out briefly from between the crates at her son who cared more for wailing these strange foreign melodies than for the tradition of his fathers. Past the Store, which no longer seemed like an armed fortress of the opposition but a house of a man struggling to understand his world.

Past the noodle stall, where the mah-jongg game clicked, drowning out the song momentarily . . . past the boiler room of the rice wine factory, where the green eyes of the gas-jet ghost burned in the darkness. On past the buildings by the sea, on down to the temple and the hillside, where the tiny houses rose like patchwork under the stars. Singing, singing, singing the words of peace until they mixed with the sound of the waves and floated up to the coop perched up on the cliffs, against the cold starry sky.

"The world in solemn stillness lay, to hear the angels sing . . ."

I watched them walking along the beach, singing. Tommy had caught China Pearl's hand and was holding it gently, as though it might break. Wing was walking apart, humming a little, not really singing the words. The Jeng boys were singing as lustily as they had put the fire out the night of the Devil Festival, putting themselves wholeheartedly into whatever the occasion demanded.

Tong walked between Gordon and me, his face glowing in the reflection of the small red flashlight he carried. I caught his eye and smiled.

"Do you hear the gongs, Tong?" I asked.

He closed his eyes for a moment, and smiled, taking a long breath.

"All the gongs are one sound," he said. "This Festival of Peace is a festival of all people. Call it what name you will, I have felt it in a part of my heart that does not lie."

When they had all gone home that night, we lit our trusty red candle, now almost burned to a stub, and stared into it, too full to talk.

I wanted to ask Gordon if he felt it too, if he had not felt Christmas more deeply on this unlikely street than on any of the streets of our childhood, with spice and snow and all the right people, and if this were not proof that we should stay here forever in this wild and wonderful place.

But we both stared into the candle, neither of us trusting ourselves to words.

We carried the flickering stub upstairs and checked that the children were covered for the night. Deidra in her straight, composed, ladylike sleep; Marita sprawled like a bird in flight; Mike curled up tightly with his pillow between his knees; and Chris with his long eyelashes drooped on round rosy cheeks. And we knew they were the greatest gift we could ever give each other—and a sacred trust.

Then we carried the candle up to the small white room and found a note on our pillow, scribbled by the girls and signed with both their names:

We hope you enjoyed showing the village kids what Christmas is about.

I picked up the note and laid it aside.

Wang Tai was right, as usual. To keep peace at home was the most difficult task, even harder than peace on earth.

The candle finally sputtered and went out, and we lay together in the darkness, full of bittersweetness and the sound of the sea.

dance
of the dragon

For months we had been asking to see Tong's paintings with the intention of buying one, but he had never showed them to us. Now with Chinese New Year coming and the necessity to earn extra cash, he brought an armload over.

He came to the door, barefoot as usual, in spite of the cold weather. The most I had ever seen on Tong's feet was a pair of rubber toe-thongs, even though his other clothes were chosen with care. When I had asked him why he always went barefooted, he smiled his Buddha-like smile and said he liked the feel of the earth under his feet.

He lined up the boards and canvasses against the courtyard wall, and Gordon and I looked at them, too surprised at first to venture a comment. The paintings had a wild primitive power, like Tong himself, yet they were hard to classify as a type of art. They were not the dainty kind of bamboo-and-bird or rocks-and-mountain paintings that one terms Chinese art nor were they typically Western. The heavy shapes and bright unshaded colors reminded one of a Gauguin or a Van Gogh, but on closer inspection few of them lived up to their original promise.

Tong watched our expressions, eager for a response.

"He helps me, this Anglissman," he said. "If I do something wrong, he teaches me. He shows me how to do it better."

"Is he an artist?" Gordon asked.

"Haih, he's a very good artist. He gets a lot of money for his paintings. That's why I let him show me how."

I picked up a small painting of boats drawn up on the beach.

"This one is interesting," I said. "Is it here in the village?"

"Ah, that one," he smiled. "You like it? I sat on a rooftop and painted the boats, then I showed it to my boss, the Anglissman, and he told me to change it. See here, where the boats were too wide—he told me make them different."

So that was it. Tong's art was not coming out as he envisioned it. Someone was changing his work.

"You shouldn't be so easily influenced," I said. "I'd like to see the boats the way you had them the first time. I think a broad bold boat there would have looked good."

Tong looked at me searchingly, a light rising in his eyes.

"You think so? Ah yah, I always listen to this Anglissman. He makes a lot of money, and I think if I listen to him I will be a good artist like him, and besides, he's my boss, and I have to listen to him."

"What kind of work do you do for him?" Gordon asked.

Tong looked uncomfortable.

"Ah, just sweep the floor and do whatever he asks me. Sometimes just keep him company. He . . . this Anglissman is not a very good man, according to our Chinese way of thinking. He is very strange, this Anglissman."

Tong paused, and the way he said Angliss sounded like a combination of anger and anguish, with a touch of something else thrown in.

"He never has women servants, only boys in his house." Tong glanced at me, unsure as to how much it was proper to say in my presence. "Many times I say I won't go back there because I hate this man, but then I need the money, and always I hope he will teach me more how to paint, and he has good friends, big friends who will buy pictures. Always I hope I can sell some pictures, so I go back."

Tong's face was red, and his eyes were glassy.

"What do you call this one?" Gordon asked, picking up a canvas with bright explosions of color splashed across undulating lines.

"Ah, that one. That is what I see inside my head when I go to the hospital and get the electric shocks."

96

"Why must you do that?"

"Ayie, sometimes there is too much bad in my head, too much angry, and I think maybe I will kill somebody, and then I go to the hospital, and they help me forget."

We bought a leaf print that Tong had done from leaves picked up on the mountainside behind our house, and he was happy.

"Someday paint the picture again with broad boats," I said. "I'd like to see it!"

He promised he would.

It was cold, drizzly February weather, typical of Chinese New Year in Hong Kong. The dusty streets of the village had washed to mud, and the mud had washed to the sea, leaving the market clean and cold. Bright conical piles of oranges lighted the cold dark shadows of the street. Rows of tiny kumquat trees in brown earthen pots stood ready for sale, and the shops were filled with dried fruits and candied vegetables to celebrate the festival.

Wong Tai came bustling to our house, and after several cups of tea and commiseration about the cost of things at New Year, reminded me that household help received double wages at New Year.

"But only half of double, since she only worked for you a half year," she instructed. "And most people expect to get a raise, even if it's only a small one. It's a loss of face not to get a raise at New Year, and people who don't, take it as a sign they're not wanted and look for work elsewhere."

I knew most of this protocol from former years in Hong Kong but thanked Wong Tai for her reminder. The thought of doing without Ah Wai at this point left me terrified. Even the week she had asked to have off at Chinese New Year was going to be a hardship. How had I ever imagined I could get along here without help?

A notice came from the Store saying it would be closed for three days, and all customers should stock up on necessary items for that period of time. I made a list and went down the street to shop.

It was strange to relate to Hong Sang as a friend, and both of us felt shy and ill at ease. There was a self-conscious smile on his face now, instead of the look of icy courtesy he had always reserved for us, and a compulsion to make conversation now, where silence had been enough before.

"Do you celebrate the New Year at your house?" he asked.

"We try," I laughed. "We need people to tell us how, because we feel ignorant of many of the customs."

He nodded and smiled.

"You have many friends in the village," he said. "They will teach you."

I glanced down at the counter beside Hong Sang and saw his little daughter, a child of five or six, sitting on top of it, coloring on a piece of paper. I had seen her in the Store before but had never looked at her closely. Her features were delicately carved and her eyes were bright, but her skin was deathly pale.

"Can you write your name?" I asked her.

The child turned away and hid her face against her father.

"Please excuse her for being shy," Hong Sang apologized. "She must stay home with her mother much of the time because she has a sickness, a sickness in her blood."

"I'm sorry. What a shame!" I said, and at that moment seeing the pain on his face, I wondered why I had ever thought of Hong Sang as anything less than deeply human.

In the house on the corner by the sea, we were almost as excited about the coming festival as if we had been Chinese. Ah Wai, in gratitude for her raise, bought a kumquat tree as a gift to our family, and it sat in the entryway, splendid and golden on a blue chest. Gordon brought home bags of dried fruits, candied carrots and melon, shaved sweet coconut, peanut brittle and roasted watermelon seeds to serve with tea to callers during the holidays. These, with a plentiful stock of Jasmine and Tit-gon-yum were placed in the kitchen in preparation for the celebration of the Lunar New Year.

The night before New Year, *Nin Sa'maan,* Gordon went to the flower market to buy a ready-to-bloom peach tree for the living room, and we carefully filled red lucky packets with coins for the children and unmarried. Like every other household on the street, we were prepared.

Our children demanded to stay up all night so they could see themselves grow an inch, like the Chinese children, but by eleven o'clock they had fallen asleep in heaps on the floor and had to be carried to bed.

We had told them the story of Jo Gwan, the kitchen god, who on this night had his lips sealed with honey, so that when he rose up to the sky in the night to report the doings of the family for the old year to the heavenly headquarters, he would say only sweet words.

"That's silly," Marita said. "How could a little wooden carving float up to the sky?"

"Well how could a big fat man float down from the sky at Christmastime?" DeDe argued. "Of course it's silly. A lot of things that people think are silly, but they still believe them."

I listened to them, wondering if observing the customs of two cultures would rob their ability to believe implicitly in either one of them.

When the children were asleep, we looked out over the street and saw the lights flickering as each family gathered around the New Year feast, each family complete, as the year of the Cock expired.

And we wondered what we would learn from this most important of Chinese holidays.

The day dawned bright and clear, bringing in the year of the Dog. The street was quiet, and the shops were closed, while everyone slept off the feast of the night before. On the edge of the beach, all twenty-one fishing boats were anchored. They bobbed lazily on the blue morning sea, their dark grey timbers aflutter with red strips of paper announcing good luck and prosperity for the New Year.

In the house on the corner, we missed the sound of the pig carts. It was so quiet that this one morning when it was legitimate, it was impossible to sleep.

Gordon rolled over and gave me a sleepy grin.

"Aren't you supposed to get up and serve me tea this morning like a good obedient wife?" he asked.

"So what else is new?" I responded sleepily.

"Only make it coffee."

"Not on your life. You've got to play it straight, or I'm not getting up."

"Then I'll have coffee after the tea."

"How about mixing them together?"

"That's a little more intercultural than I could take."

We were hardly up before Tommy was at the door.

"Gung Hei Faat Choy! Congratulations and Prosperity," he called happily, clasping his hands and bowing slightly.

"Gung Hei Faat Choy!" we all echoed, and Gordon reached for two red lucky packets to place in his hands.

Chris ran around in excited circles.

"Gung Hei Faat Choy, where's my money, Gung Hei Faat Choy, where's my money?" he shouted.

Tommy caught him up and hoisted him to his shoulder, dancing around the room with the little boy.

"Why do you say congratulations?" Mike wanted to know.

"Congratulations to you, for being alive, Miko!" Tommy answered. "And may your life be successful!"

There was another knock, and Wing was at the door.

"The Dragon Dance is coming in a few minutes," he said excitedly. "My younger brother will be dancing the lead part this morning."

We heard the beating of gongs and the shouting of a crowd and ran out the door. From where we stood on the corner, we could see the procession coming. The main dancer was dressed in black pants and white shirt. He held the creature's gaudily painted head, leaping, bending, jumping, and shaking to the rhythm of the gongs. Other dancers carried the tail, and a tambourine player baited the creature along.

The gongs pounded wildly, and the creature leapt in the air and came down with the agility of a big cat.

"Is it really a lion or a dragon?" I shouted to Tommy above the noise.

"It doesn't matter," he said, shrugging his shoulders happily. "It's a Kei-Leun, in Chinese, but there is no such animal, so you can call it whatever you like."

"Then it isn't a dragon?"

"It can be a dragon if you like," he said agreeably.

The street was packed with people who seemed to have materialized out of the silence a short time before. Everyone was dressed in bright new clothes: men in blue padded jackets or Western suits, and women in colorful padded silk jackets and dark pants. The children were rosy-cheeked and laughing, decked out in bright red jackets with pink or orange ribbons in the girls' black hair. Everyone was smiling and calling greetings to someone.

The jostling crowd engulfed us and swept us into the street. It took us past the boarded-up market stalls and down the far end of the wine factory street to the Jeng's rice shop. They came out smiling and calling greetings and joined the crowd, and we moved on. There was a press of bodies, a movement as of one living organism, and no one turned and apologized for touching another.

The lion-dragon led the crowd on, dancing and leaping, bowing and shaking, low and high, up and down. I watched this celebration of life, this welcome to a new year of being that would follow its patterns of height and depth, complexities and joys.

I looked up and saw we were near the lion-dragon. The face of Wing's younger brother peered out from under the mask.

"Ding Tai, Ding Sang, Gung Hei Faat choy!" said the lion-dragon. "I'll be at your house to drink tea this afternoon."

I blinked, a bit shaken. It was the first time a *Kei-Luen* had ever spoken to me.

Then he bent down, jumped up and shook his magical tail, and was off again to the beating of the gong. I wondered if I were hearing things and decided I would know if the mythical creature came for tea.

At the other end of the street, tiny children were imitating the dance. A small dragon only about two feet tall was jumping and shaking its tail ferociously while a miniature tambourine-shaker hopped about. The tradition was being passed on.

Later that afternoon, we decided to climb the mountainside and visit Mok Tai. The Kei-Leun had come for tea, along with one of the Mok boys, who had extended Mok Tai's invitation to come to her house to wish her a happy New Year. After the social blunder with Wong Tai at the Moon Festival, we were anxious to start the New Year right.

Halfway up the mountain Wing joined us, and the five of us picked our way through the tarpaper shacks, chicken yards, and pig pens to a stone stairway leading up the side of a knoll. The stones were moss-covered and sunken deep into the hillside, giving one the feeling of climbing over a natural rock formation.

Mok Tai was waiting for us, bowing and smiling. I entered the house with a feeling of reserved anticipation, ready to accept whatever squalid conditions we met as a part of the hillside, a part of a regrettable condition.

But what we actually saw was so unexpected that it totally unnerved me. The house was built into the hillside, following the contours of boulders and earth. The small main room and the bedrooms were plastered grey and decorated with bright red New Year sayings inscribed in black ink. One entire end of the main room was banked with growing flowers, a wild burst of reds and pinks, whites and purples. The floor was earthen, pounded brown and swept smooth as tile. In the open space adjacent to the main room, a stone fireplace was freestanding on the floor, and earthen pots sat over the grating, blackened with swirling patterns of soot.

The beauty of their house made me feel ashamed of my readiness to accept those who were less fortunate than I and made me wonder again what was more and what was less, how beauty and worth are measured. I wanted to kneel and confess to someone what a snob I still was, after all these years, always ready to condescend, to accept as the knowing one when there was so much more for me to know. I wanted to take this room and all its simple uncluttered way, its magnetic earthy power and let it make me something I was becoming but was not yet.

Mok Tai would have been terrified if I had knelt on her floor and said what was on my mind. We politely drank her tea and tried her delicacies and left our gift of oranges. Then we bowed out through the door where hung the words *Go and Come in Peace.*

Go and come in the peace of discovering unexpected beauty . . . and wherever you find beauty, take it into yourself . . . you are a part of it.

We made our way back down the mountain, the boys again showing us the intricacies of the path. Gordon kept up a lively conversation with the Wong boy about who lived where and who was related to whom, and I walked along behind. Children laughed at us and pointed chubby fingers at our Western faces, dogs barked, and adults gazed at us curiously, then melted into friendly smiles when we greeted them in Chinese.

I surveyed the hillside, a mass of thoughts crowding through my mind as complex as the patchwork pattern of rooftops spread below us. They were thoughts unbidden, uncensored, rising to question my white middle class background.

I wondered why I was more comfortable if I could view myself as being more fortunate than someone else, why I needed to look down on someone, even if ever so discreetly, before I felt secure.

I wondered why scenes of sickness or poverty or hunger caused my adrenalin to flow faster than pictures of soundness and health.

And I wondered why it is so difficult to accept people as they are and why it was so easy to want to change them so that they resembled me. And I thought of how the compulsion to change others is a form of nonacceptance. And how we classify others as poor or hungry or naked and need to be insulated against them by the distance of a gift. And how even the seemingly gracious compulsion to give can be a form of nonacceptance.

Then the wrenching question of how one reconciles the need for accepting people as they are with the honest need for change.

At that point I wondered if I could accept every person on that hillside as a valid human being, a living miracle, as a creation of God, how it would affect my feeling toward their needs.

I gazed down over the patchwork of rooftops, smelled the stench of pig pens and poor sanitation, and I knew it was a part of me, that the people who lived here were a part of the same life that I was a part of, and their way of being was not a thing aside from me. If this hillside were a good way of being, it was good for me; if this were poverty, then I too was poor. If I thought of it as having nothing to do with me, I was broken.

Accept and take this stench of poverty into you. Whatever happens here affects you, affects the whole world. Nothing is of itself.

But how can I accept this? How would Yeso, born at the Holy Birth Festival, have looked at this hillside? Would he have loved the people and hated the stench? What sign did my people have to help me deal with this? The cross? What did the cross have to say to this?

I wondered, but there was no answer.

On the second day of the New Year, Tommy had a pocketful of lucky money and insisted on taking us to a village teahouse for lunch. We started to refuse but saw a hint of rejection in his eyes, as though we were referring to the fact that he could not afford such luxuries.

"It's New Year, and we have to celebrate!" he smiled brightly. "I eat so much food at your house, now you must come with me."

We went to the teahouse across from the bus stop. It was gaily decorated with red dragons and golden phoenixes and filled with noontime celebrators of the New Year. Entire families filled round tables, from the tiniest rosy youngster stuffed into his padded silk coat to the black-clad grandmothers with coiffed grey hair in a neat bun. Always the grandmothers looked old and dignified, never pseudo-young. The very old wore traditional black velvet caps.

Tommy seated the six of us around a table and ordered hot tea. "Do you like dim sum?" he asked.

We did. Often we had come to Chinese restaurants where dim sum was served, the steamed bamboo dishes of assorted foods brought around by young waiters, and chosen at the table according to the customer's taste.

"Can we have spring rolls?" the children begged. They were counting the lucky money they had accumulated in the walk through the market.

"How about steamed shrimp balls, Ha Gow?" Tommy suggested.

"You order," said Gordon, "and we'll be satisfied."

Tommy filled our glasses with steaming tea, and we cupped the amber tumblers in our hands, grateful for their warmth in the unheated restaurant. No place was ever heated in the village. Even weather just short of freezing was accepted as a natural thing, a day to wear more sweaters but certainly not a call to heat the house.

There was a wistful look on Tommy's face as he looked around at the family groupings in the restaurant.

"My father came home yesterday," he said quietly, his words almost lost in the uproar of the teahouse.

Gordon looked at Tommy quickly.

"I thought I saw him on the street. Does he look very much like you?"

"I hope not," Tommy said, toying with his glass. "I don't want to be like him. I don't have as much respect for my father as a Chinese boy should have."

"Why is that?"

"A good Chinese father should take care of his family. My father is always gone and leaves my mother to raise the children. I have to worry about helping to earn money, about my little brother who can't go to school, about my sister growing up on the street. I have no time to be young. If he can't live with us the rest of the year, I don't care for him to come home at New Year. What meaning does it have?"

"But why doesn't he live at home? Your father and mother—"

"No, it's not a marriage thing. It's a matter of face." Tommy paused and looked around to see who was sitting at the adjoining tables. He bent over and spoke quietly to us, a precaution hardly necessary in the din of the restaurant. "My father and mother used to own this teahouse," he said, "and he was a very big man in the village, one of the leaders of the Kai Fong."

Tommy lapsed into a moody silence, as though he had said enough. I thought of Yau Tai, housed in her knocked-together shelter, working among the crates of vegetables, and wondered what had happened.

Chinese New Year would not have been a holiday to the young bloods of Check Wan without a village dance. China Pearl and Tommy, Tong and Wing, the Jeng boys and the Mok boys, along with assorted Wongs and Chuns decided to plan a youth-sponsored dance at the only place in the village large enough for such an activity, the maternity home.

Gordon and I laughed when we heard it.

"The maternity home?" I asked. "There's nothing like holding a dance with a built-in warning system!"

But Tommy was oblivious to the joke. He thought we meant it would disturb the mothers who were in residence.

"There's nobody there this time of year," he assured us. "Most Chinese babies are conceived during New Year. Nine months from now is the big baby season!"

The boys began to plan refreshments, and for some reason, Tommy thought that potato salad was the most exciting food that could be served at a dance. I suggested baked finger foods, but he insisted on making potato salad.

The day of the dance I helped him boil pans of potatoes, and we bought salad dressing from Hong Sang, chopped onions, eggs, and celery until we had a huge red plastic dishpan full of potato salad. Tommy viewed it with evident satisfaction.

"That will be right," he said. "We're doing Western dancing and we must eat Western food."

"Even at Chinese New Year?"

"We're the new generation," he said. "We have to learn how to mix customs. Tell Marita, Mike, and Deidra they're invited to the dance too. We need more girls. Most of the people in our group are boys because the village mothers don't like their girls to come."

We told the children of the invitation, and they decided, hesitatingly, to go. Their exposure to other Western children at the American school was making them self-conscious about their village friends, and the relationship between them and the village was not as free and open as it had once been. Some days when they came home from school, Wing's sister Mei Ho would be waiting to play with them, but when she saw they had brought along other Western friends, she would exclaim in alarm, "Ah yah, they've brought some little devils with them. I'm going home!" And the relationships began to be strained.

But a dance at the maternity home with potato salad for refreshments sounded like fun, and they decided to go.

I watched them run out the door that night, realizing that Marita would be twelve in the summer and that she was suddenly becoming tall and pretty. Her blond blue-eyed looks stood out in stark contrast to the dark handsome young people of the village, and I began to think about the future. There had been a time when I considered Asians as something quite apart, when I hardly considered an Asian man as a genuine male. But since living in the village, this feeling had changed, and I felt the warmth and humanness of every person deeply. They were no longer grocery boys or carpenters or little men who sold vegetables. They were live vibrant human beings with hearts and passions like all the people I had known; I began to wonder how I would feel if Marita or Deidra would grow up and fall in love with a Chinese boy. I closed my eyes and thought of Tommy or Wing or one of the Jeng boys as a son-in-law, and it made me stop and think twice. For the boys themselves, accepting them would be easy. I already loved them as persons. But what about the complicated maze of family that stood behind every individual? What about Tommy's mother and her strict adherence to the old Buddhist ways, her almost fanatical belief in ghosts and devils. What about her house? Could I face the fact that my daughter's mother-in-law lived in packing crates, that they would not be able to communicate easily in the same language, that my daughter would be considered a white devil wherever she went until it was explained that she was one of the family? It was not just the two people involved but two cultures that came to bear on the one fragile point of contact between these two people.

And what if Mike grew up to marry a Chinese? I had seen them walking down the street often, the tall Western men with their tiny Chinese brides, and I always resented it . . . somehow threatening to me to have a man of my race choose a woman of another race, almost like a personal rejection. It was as though they had something that was almost forbidden, almost illegal, and certainly more exotic than the ordinary couple; I knew that this was a depth of acceptance I had to nourish as much as any Chinese mother on the village street.

Then I comforted myself that Marita and Mike were only eleven, and such fears would resolve themselves as time went along. Yau Tai, or any other mother in the village, would probably be horrified at the thought of a Western daughter-in-law.

They came home from the dance, aglow with fun and innocent laughter, and I knew they were still children, able to relate in a beautiful way to the gentle youth of Check Wan village.

On the fifth day of the New Year, the Jeng boys came to our house.

"Our mother wants to invite you for dinner tonight," they said. "If she invites you, would you come?"

I wondered if Jeng Tai, too, had heard of the Moon Festival invitation and wanted to play safe before losing face by a refusal.

"We would be honored," we said.

The boys went to tell their mother and came back in less than half an hour.

"She invites you to come," they said politely.

"At what time?"

"What time do you usually eat?"

"Around six."

"Six will be a good time."

At a little before six, we made our way down the wine factory street, between the high stone walls, past the noodle shop, and down to the rice shop. Most of the places of business were still closed for the New Year festival. Even at the Jengs, the iron grating was pulled over the wooden shutters, and we had to knock to enter.

The boys welcomed us through a section of the grating just wide enough to squeeze in one person at a time. We filed past the covered rice barrels and on to the back of the store where burlap sacks of rice were stacked to the ceiling.

It was dark inside the shop, with one light bulb hanging from the ceiling shaded by a newspaper. The wood of the old beams was dark and ancient, and the smell of burlap and salt-water filled the air.

One small table was set up in the middle of the floor, and I began to wonder how all fourteen of us would sit at one small folding table.

Jeng Tai came out of the kitchen, her face red from bending over the fire. She was beaming and ordering everyone around.

"China Pearl, pour Ding Tai and Ding Sang some tea. Welcome, welcome! My husband is still at a mah-jongg game he's been playing all day. You have to let these men gamble a little money at New Year's time . . . he hasn't come back yet. Ah yah, sit down, sit down and drink some tea. Eldest Son, get some *Ho-Lok*, some Coke for the children."

She hurried back into the kitchen where the rich aroma of garlic and ginger mixed with soy sauce and rice wine smelled delicious.

The dishes began to arrive on the table, but Jeng Sang was not home yet, so no one sat down. We stood talking to the Jeng boys while China Pearl and her mother produced one dish after another and deposited them on the table. I watched the chicken with mushroom soup, the sauteed prawns, the steamed fish, thinking how nervous I would be if I were putting all this on the table when my husband had not appeared, but Jeng

Tai seemed as cheerful as if nothing were happening. The Jeng boys kept slipping out the door one by one to remind their father to come, but he was busy in his game and in no hurry.

In the center of the bamboo shoots and mushrooms, the fried bean curd and steamed fish, there appeared a platter of french fries and a bottle of catsup.

"We didn't know what your children would like," China Pearl explained, tossing her long hair. "We thought they might like these."

"Oh, our children eat anything!" I said confidently. I was rather sure they would, since we had had a ten-minute instruction session on this just before leaving the house.

Jeng Sang was still out playing mah-jongg, and we all stood around the table, letting the food get cold. The boys stood and talked to us, patient for hungry boys, and I began to form a different impression of Jonathan, the eldest Jeng boy. He had seemed like a simple unthinking child last fall and even during the Christmas celebration, but somehow with the passing of the weeks, he had begun to grow up. To pass the time and keep our minds off the chilling food, Gordon talked with him.

"Is this a New Year saying?" Gordon asked him, pointing to a wooden plaque on a wall post, facing the street.

"No," said Jonathan. "That's a good-luck writing. When my father bought this shop many years ago, he had a wise man come and tell him if the location were good, if it lay right with the wind and the water, the *Fung-Sui*. The man said it was all fine except for this post, because it cuts right in the middle of the shop facing us. So he wrote these words on the wall to correct the problem."

"And now it's all right?"

The boy looked at Gordon and smiled, then scraped his toe across the floor shyly.

"Of course, I don't believe this," he said apologetically. "We younger people have been educated. You'll have to excuse my parents. They are uneducated country people."

"But in spite of your Western education, you must have heard many stories and legends as a child," I injected. "Did you think of them as being real when you heard them?"

"Of course, for a long time I did. All children accept things as the truth when they first hear them, because children are innocent and trusting. And then you understand one day that these things cannot be true, because the world is not that way. And then as you think about it more, you know that there is a kind of truth in the stories and legends that say something about life. Then you can refer to the stories and quote the sayings, but they have a different meaning for you. You realize they are not true or untrue in the usual sense, but they contain something true."

I listened, fascinated by this young boy's analysis of his culture.

"What would be an example of this?" I asked.

He thought for a moment, scraping his toe over the floor.

"It's like the goddess Tin Hau, the Heaven Queen, protector of the sea people. In old times, many people thought it was dangerous to rescue drowning people from the sea—even if a child fell in, no one would rescue him because it was believed if someone fell in they had somehow angered the goddess, and the life of the one who rescued him would be demanded as a payment; Tin Hau's actions were not to be questioned. But now this idea is going away. Modern lifeguards are coming to the beaches, and her name is taken on by them. There is even a Tin Hau temple that is considered the special temple of lifeguards who work at the beaches. They have become the protectors of the people who swim; they save people in the name of the goddess, changing the old superstition to something useful."

"Then you think this attitude is not only for you but for a whole generation of people as well?" I asked.

"I hope so. You never can tell when people will fall back into their old superstitions when they are frightened or in trouble. But I know, for me—" he motioned to the wooden plaque on the beam, "—I will never hang up such lucky words in my house, or if I do, it will only be as a reminder of old things and not anything I believe in to bring me luck."

Tommy squeezed in through the crack in the railing, and I saw he had been invited for dinner. He was scrubbed and polished, with his hair slicked down and his best clothes on.

Jeng Tai was bustling about, calling us to the table, finally deciding to eat without Jeng Sang. She scolded the ginger-striped cat and the two dogs, said that her house was old, ugly, and dirty and there was nothing on the table to eat; then over our assurances that it was a beautiful house, very well-kept and that we had never seen so much food at once, she settled us on the stools.

First the six of our family were seated, with Chris on my lap, then Tommy, China Pearl, and all the various sizes of Jeng boys formed a second outer ring around the table, reaching their chopsticks between our shoulders. Jeng Tai ladled out steaming portions of rice, and it was hardly noticed that the other dishes had cooled off. It was the first time I had ever seen fifteen people seated around one small card table, but it worked, knee-to-knee and shoulder-to-shoulder. It was even a good way to keep warm.

Jeng Sang finally came, looking like a tall hollow-cheeked Asian Lincoln, and was absorbed into the table with greetings and murmurs of "A-Pa, eat rice," from the boys as a token of respect. He seemed to be a tremendously proud man and surrounded by seven sturdy sons, a beautiful daughter, a good business, and an obedient wife, who could blame him?

At the coming of the man of the house, Jeng Tai brought out a shiny new bottle of brandy, poured it straight into tall water glasses with a glug-glug sound, and sat one at each adult's place.

Gordon looked at me, and I looked at him. Neither of us dared to tackle a whole water tumbler full of straight brandy.

"Come on, Dad," DeDe reminded us, sensing our hesitation. "You said eat whatever was put in front of you, and that means drinks too. *Ouch*, who did that?"

I had kicked her under the table before she disclosed too many more vital facts, such as the matter that all our children thought we were hopelessly old-fashioned because neither of us smoked or drank like most of their friends' parents did.

The Jeng boys who understood English glanced at us, and Jeng Tai glanced at them for an explanation.

"Is something wrong with the drink?" she asked, sniffing the bottle. "It cost over ten dollars. It's a Western drink. If it's bad I'll take it back and get another one. The store is open—"

"No, no!" Gordon said quickly. "This drink is fine! There's no problem with the drink. It's just that we don't know how to enjoy it; we don't know how to drink so *much* of it!"

Her face dissolved in relief.

"Ah, Ding Sang! So polite! You are too polite! Drink! Drink all of it. This is a celebration, and you have given me much face by eating in our humble home tonight. Drink!"

It was a choice between ruining a friendship or drinking the brandy.

We sipped it, warm and strong and bitter, and she beamed and bustled about the table. Chris chased the ginger cat through the burlap sacks while the older children ate bean curd and abalone and seaweed, and we all stepped into never-never land in the rice shop, with the rough beams and the sea at the back door.

And I began to feel the dragon dancing in my head and knew that total acceptance, like straight brandy, could warm the heart and blur the judgment . . . that it was a dangerous life-substance which could create and destroy.

On the sixth day, wide-eyed students from Gordon's school came to pay their respects to the headmaster. They sat for hours talking with Gordon, while they ate watermelon seeds and dropped the husks on the floor. The depth of their respect seemed to be measured by the length of time they sat. There were dark-haired boys who wanted us to put on tapes so they could dance, and shy little girls with soup-bowl haircuts who sat and giggled while they carefully covered their teeth.

Sometimes the boys invited us to dance with them. They showed us dances that we had been out of our own culture too long to know, Western dances that these sharp young students of the new world had picked up from movies and television.

But some of the students sat in the corner giggling and were content to sip tea and eat seeds and cover their teeth because their parents did not like the Western dances and had forbidden them to make a show of themselves in public.

It was the seventh day of the New Year, the birthday of all people. Chun Tai's baby, born only a few months before and considered a year old when she was born, on this day became two years old. Individual birthdays were recorded, but the condition of being born was only celebrated on the seventh day of the New Year. Not until one was sixty was one's full life celebrated in an individual birthday.

All during the celebration of the New Year, the matter of acceptance had been with me. I saw people who were not in what would be called comfortable circumstances celebrating the coming of this New Year with an openness and joy that was deeper than any acceptance of life I had ever seen, life with all its harshness and even failure.

But how much more there was to learn from our Chinese friends about the intricacies of acceptance never occurred to me until this seventh day when I took the bus to the downtown area of Hong Kong. Since it was the last day of the celebration, the buses were crowded with people out visiting their friends and relatives. Getting on at the downtown terminal, I had a seat, but by the time the bus reached the second stop, people were standing.

Two young men boarded the bus, one quite intoxicated, and the other only feeling good. It was such a rarity to see a young Chinese drunk in the downtown area that I stared at him quite openly. As a reward for my undivided attention, he came and stood over my seat, hanging on to the overhead railing and breathing down my neck.

I looked around at the other passengers, wondering to whom I could turn if he became obnoxious, but they did not seem to see him.

"You'd better not go to his house so drunk," said the more sober one. "He'll think you're a fool!"

"Hah! I'm not afraid of your old uncle. *Diu* him and diu his old mother."

I looked around again to see if anyone were shocked by his obscene language. No one moved.

"When I invite you out to drink, you don't have to drink so much."

"Hah! Then don't invite me next time. Diu you and diu your old mother."

"Hush! Don't open your mouth and talk so coarsely. There are women—"

"Hah! Women! Who, this old foreign devil bag?" he said, leaning close over me. "Diu your old mother. She doesn't know what I'm saying, she doesn't know how to listen to us."

It was too much of a temptation. I looked up at him and in rapid Cantonese said, "I do too know what you're saying, and I've heard just about enough."

He peered down at me as if he were seeing a ghost.

"Wah," he said wonderingly. "Diu your old mother. A man can't even swear in peace these days without having some foreign devil understand what he's saying. Diu you—" he hung onto the overhead bar and said it like a benediction, weaving sleepily on his heels.

The other passengers looked straight ahead, neither hearing nor seeing. In their minds this was not taking place because it was not supposed to take place. Any deviation from acceptable behavior was only temporary and as long as no one was hurt, would pass away if everyone ignored it. One must smile and wait patiently for a foolish young brother to learn a lesson.

I felt the group on the bus surrounding him with a subtle acceptance, a pressure to conform by refusing to *see* him when he did not conform to acceptable behavior.

The days of that month passed, days when I was stunned by poverty and shocked by beauty, days when my ears were filled with new things, both beautiful and terrible. And always there was the knowing that to be cut off from anything that was happening, to count it outside myself, was to be less than whole, less than a true part of God.

Walls within walls came tumbling down, and even the invisible barriers fell, and the child born crippled was my child, and the heart broken was my heart, and every happening, good or evil, was a part of the life of God in me, struggling to be accepted if not understood.

This largeness was like an ocean, and I was adrift in it. I could not hate anyone without having it turn to self-hate. It frightened me, this largeness, even more than the smallness I had despised because I no longer had any orderly compartments of right and wrong, of yes and no. And in this open largeness, who knew what evil ghosts lurked? If the whole of life was God, who and what was evil? How could I deal with evil, even know what it was?

Sometimes as I walked the streets, there were things I could not accept because to accept them violated my sense of worth, the worth of every person. At the corner across from the noodle shop was a covered area where all sorts of toys were displayed, mostly cheap plastic toys made in Hong Kong. At first I wondered why this shop was frequented by young British soldiers from a nearby fort, and then I saw a table inside where cans of beer were served and heard the juke box that blared rock-and-roll. Moving among the soldiers was a young girl, the daughter of the shop owner. The soldiers made coarse jokes about her, and put their hands on her, and treated her as one more cheap plastic toy.

Sometimes I met her on the street and smiled, and saw her face growing tough and vacant, robbed of the open softness the village girls possessed. She filled me with a kind of terror, like a wild animal that had been wounded and left to hop about helplessly.

One time I asked Wing Sung about her. He shook his head and lowered his eyes.

"It's pitiful," he said. "But one must find money to eat, is it not so?"

And then there were the resident heroin addicts on the hillside behind our house. Gordon was concerned about them and asked Tommy about them.

"Ah, leave them alone, they're harmless." Tommy smiled. "Once in a while they need money for buying the poison, so they steal a little. No one else in the village steals. How could I take your shirt? If I did, you would see me wear it! So if we miss something, we go up to the poison-eaters' shed to see if they have taken it. If they still have it, they give it back. If it has been sold, what can be done?"

"But the men are on heroin. Doesn't anyone care about them?"

Tommy shrugged his shoulders.

"If a man decides to waste his life, who can stop him?" he said.

One day I noticed a strange child riding on the pig carts. His hair was sandy brown and fine, instead of jet black and coarse like the other children. His eyes were flecked with brownish-green, and his complexion, although tan from the out-of-doors, did not have the golden tint that the other toddlers had.

I asked Ah Wai who this child was.

"Ah yah, that one. He's the grandson of a woman who lives on the hillside. She sent her daughter to work for a Western family. The girl was young and had no knowledge of such matters, so when the husband of the family began to speak kindly to her, she did not know to be afraid. Then the wife went away, and he took the girl to his bed, telling her he preferred her to his wife. The girl thought he would marry her and perhaps some day she could go to his country, but when he knew she would have this child, the man put her out and acted like he never knew her."

"Did the girl tell his wife?"

"Hah, what good would that do? Make more trouble? No, there was trouble enough, so the girl came back here to the hillside and had her baby quietly. Now the grandmother takes care of it, and the girl has gone back to work in another place."

"How does the grandmother feel about the child?"

"Ayie, it is hard to say. A child is a child, and it is half of her own daughter. But the blood has been mixed, has been ruined, and the hair and eyes are not right. It is a shame to her household. It is like having a half-devil in the house."

"But he's a very handsome little boy!"

"Handsome in whose eyes? The Chinese will say he is half-devil, and the Westerners will say he is half-Chinese. Who will accept such a child?"

"But it's a new day. People's minds are not so narrow anymore."

"Hearts are very narrow. What you know in your mind, you cannot always feel in your heart. A child like this will suffer loneliness all his life if he stays in this village. Ah yah, and such a pity. What did he have to do with being born?"

Her eyes filled with tears, and she brushed them aside with the back of her hand. Looking at her time-worn face, I understood that even the most accepting person finds some things unacceptable because they hurt and destroy without the consent of those who are hurt.

I began to have a deep fear, a sense of panic that with acceptance came a loss of control, that life was an indiscriminate force, which did its blind dance, creating here and destroying there without reason, conceiving and bearing the child of deceit and abuse as automatically as the child of love and care.

And I wondered where, in the openness of acceptance, there was a correspondingly larger safety, how and where it had anything to do with the love of God, the Creator of life, and I determined not to leave this street until I had found the answer to that question.

In fact, the possibility of ever deserting this street had almost left my mind. Where else in the world could one encounter and begin to understand the Dance of the Dragon?

a sip of
snake wine

The March winds had begun to blow over the village streets, and the market threw off its winter chill. Our children came home from school, impatient with winter uniforms, and ready to plunge into the sea for a swim.

Ah Wai looked at them askance.

"You'd better not let them go until after the fourth moon," she warned me. "We don't run into the sea with the first puff of warm wind. We wait until after the right amount of moons have passed."

I stood between her wisdom and the hot insistence of my American children, feeling they both were right and yet someone must be mistaken. Were not human thermostats universal equipment?

The school for fishermen's children in the village ran on half-day shifts. In the morning while the first half studied by droning out their recitations, a goodly number of the other half sat on our doorstep. It had become so much a part of the accepted order of things now, no one noticed. When I went out, I had learned to step high and place my feet carefully, and that was that.

The crowd on the front steps had even become a good source of playmates for Chris, who had now turned three. One morning there was a knock on the door, and three tiny girls stood solemnly on the steps.

"Tisso?" they asked hopefully.

I looked out into the courtyard where he was riding his tricycle. "Chris, the kids would like to play."

He hopped off his tricycle.

"Oh, can I go out in the street?"

"No, there are too many trucks."

"But the other kids play in the street!"

I glanced out onto the busy pavement, chugging with wine factory trucks, full of pig carts and many dogs. Just yesterday another dog had howled to its death, dying horribly under the wheels of a heavy truck. Was it Yau Tai who had said, *"I never worry about children playing in the street; they won't get hit unless it's ordained by fate, and then what could one do to stop it?"* I shivered, decided not to tempt fate, and invited all the children in to play.

I gave them crayons and papers, their favorite pastime, and let them go into the courtyard to draw and scribble. Chris began to draw a battleship with a bomber going overhead, a motif his placid older brother had taught him, and the Chinese children began to draw flowers, birds, and goldfish swimming with their tails at artistic angles, also learned from their older siblings.

Chris came to me with his bomber.

I looked at it and felt ashamed. How had he picked up this instinct for destruction, even here in the idyllic beauty of this ancient village? Had we not succeeded in removing even this youngest one from the brutality of war, the destruction that was tearing the world apart?

"That's nice, Chris," I said, "but why don't you draw something pretty? Something beautiful like your little friends make? Why don't you draw a tree or a bird or something from nature?"

He looked at me for a few seconds, hurt at my rejection of his art. Then I saw a gleam in his eye.

"Okay," he said. "I'll make a tree!"

He was gone for a few minutes, kneeling in the courtyard with his rear end up in the air and his chubby fists hard at work on the paper. When he finished, he brought it triumphantly back to me.

"I made a good one for you," he said.

"What is it?" I asked, looking at the drawing that was mostly black lines and circles, not wanting to wound his pride again. "You tell me about it!"

He settled on my knee and explained the drawing.

"This is a tree," he said, "and this is a bird sitting on a nest in the tree. Under the bird are some eggs. And this—" he grinned impishly, watching my face, "—is a snake climbing up the tree to eat the bird's eggs up!"

I laughed in spite of myself and folded him in a hug, paper and all. Perhaps at three years old one was not afraid to admit that nature had a fierce beauty, a cruel sense of humor. But at thirty-three, at forty-three? If God lived in all things, why was life so cruel?

That was the morning things began to happen, that questions too deep to handle began to arise, and that answers too sudden were forced on me. It was the beginning of a dangerous time.

China Pearl had asked to come over that morning. She no longer went to school because she felt it was not necessary. Already she knew much more than her mother in the way of things learned in books, and as the seven boys all needed school fees, she had simply dropped out. But now she was becoming restless, wondering what the future meant, wondering if she should learn some skill or look for a job downtown. Her mother was opposed to the whole idea. She feared to let her daughter loose in the maze of downtown Hong Kong, afraid that she would be tricked or taken advantage of or wrongly influenced. But China Pearl, young and beautiful, was beginning to be bored selling rice and peanut oil in the old shop by the sea, always under the vigilance of Momma.

On this morning, she wanted to sew a new dress for spring and asked if I would help her. I set up the machine and spread out the table to assist her in cutting.

We sat by the big wooden table, cutting and sewing, while she told me of her struggle to be obedient to her parents and yet to be herself.

"It's not so easy for a good Chinese girl," she said. "I love my parents, and they have always been very good to me. The boys say I'm spoiled, but I need to do something by myself."

Ah Wai was going through the dining room and caught a fragment of the conversation.

"Did you hear what happened to the Hui boy up on the mountain?" she asked significantly.

"Ah yah!" China Pearl said, her eyes big with fear. "Who has not heard it? Bad news travels fast in the village."

I sat, picking up pattern pieces, watching the emotions chase themselves across Pearl's face. There was always the danger of being too selfless, too obedient, too compliant.

The Hui boy was in his early twenties, normal, lively, fairly well-liked, and deeply in love with a village girl. But his mother did not approve of the girl. With the power of a traditional mother over her son, she forbad him to marry the girl, suggesting another instead.

The boy refused, and there was no more said about the matter. The young man became very quiet, refused to talk, and then began to refuse his rice. He sat in the house, day after day, growing thinner and thinner. There was no open word spoken against his mother, only a complete withdrawal from life.

Then one day a few weeks later, I had heard a crowd and looked out the window. On the road facing the sea, a strange figure was crawling along the ground, his legs locked in a twisted position, his arms propelling him along like a man without legs. Out of the crowd, a beach policeman stepped and ordered the man to his feet. He was helpless. The policeman tried to unfold his legs, but there was no way to unlock them. He was frozen in position. Finally a police truck had come, and they loaded the pathetic figure into it and took him home.

It was only a few days later that I had heard the siren of the police wagon wailing as it went past our house and on down the road toward the mountainside. There was a crowd outside, and Ah Wai rushed out to see what the commotion was. She came back into the house, a look of horror on her face.

"Ah yah, death," she gasped. "The fellow with the twisted legs has hanged himself. They found him this morning hanging by his neck from the roof of a shed. Ah yah, and he was such a good obedient boy, always."

I sat pinning the pattern to the last bit of cloth, knowing why this story frightened China Pearl, why it frightened all of us.

I threaded the machine in the delicate pink that China Pearl had chosen. She would look ravishing in this shade of pink, with her long black hair and tiny figure. Glancing at her I felt a twinge of insecurity, wondering if after four children and a winter of frugal living I was still attractive. It had been months since I had bought anything new, and my hair was its usual handy washbowl mop of close-clipped strands.

I heard the street noises and the little children's voices laughing in the courtyard. Such things as appearance could be seen to later. What mattered most was the meaning I was learning on this street.

Outside the pig carts rattled past. Voices and calls came floating in the open window, borne on the warm spring wind, and above it all the steady pounding of the sea, blending it into a pattern.

"We'll see how it works," Gordon had said months before, and it seemed to be working very well. Not all the problems were solved, but at least we were discovering what they were. In fact, living in the village had become such a way of life that I wondered, as I had many times, how we could ever leave it for reasons that seemed to change as the days went by. Each discovery seemed to raise another quest. First there had been the honest motive that drew us to identify with the opposite racial and socioeconomic group, to take a stand against barriers. Then there had been the shock of realizing the richness and depth contained in the village and the poverty of our own lives. And now . . . and now I felt the need for probing my own relationship to my newly discovered image of God-who-is-everywhere. If God were so vast, was he not also terrifyingly impersonal? What about the very real sense of evil that pervaded life, ready to pounce and hurt and destroy? Could I trust this new larger God to *care* what happened to me? What if I stared into the bottom of my fears and found all my magical protections empty? How could I ever face those deep hidden pockets of fear and come out clean? What was I really afraid of?

The sea pounded and the wind blew, and the sound of voices floated in from the street as we worked at the table. I knew I already owed this spot of the earth a tremendous debt of gratitude for what I might become, given time, given *enough* time.

The doorbell rang. I laid the scissors down and went to answer it. I was confronted by a strange young man, no one from the village, who handed me a legal notice. Then he tacked an identical notice on the wooden front door.

The children who had filled up the doorsteps scattered like a flock of birds, and I stared at the paper in disbelief.

YOU ARE TO EVICT THESE PREMISES BY APRIL 1
BY ORDER OF
P.T.YU, SOLICITOR FOR Y.W. ZEE

A feeling of shock, of release, of loss, of panic—a tumbled mixture of emotions bolted through me.

"But why?" I asked weakly. "What have we done wrong?"

The young messenger answered as though he were a tape prerecorded message.

"The landlord says his mother needs the house."

"Is that the real reason?"

"I'm only the messenger," he shrugged.

"But do you know the real reason?"

"I—you know the rents are going up everywhere, and I suspect it could be for a rent increase. He must legally evict you before he can ask you to sign at a higher price."

"Then this is not a real eviction notice? The man would talk price?"

"I suspect so."

"We're already paying twice as much as the family next door. How much would the rent increase?"

"Perhaps thirty percent."

I was so shocked I forgot to offer him tea, and he left.

Thirty percent. I followed him out the door and ripped the notice in half and threw it into the open gutter. Then I picked it up and decided to throw it in the garbage. Then I was afraid the garbage collectors would see it, so I shredded it into tiny bits and flushed it down the toilet.

We were going to be charged an exorbitant rent by some absentee landlord because we were foreigners. It was like being black on a white street, only we were pink on a yellow street. And what good did it do us to try to live here and prove the interrelatedness of mankind when the landlord did not get the point? To him the point was to squeeze us for all we were worth.

I called Gordon at the school office. His reaction was swift unbelief.

"Evicted? You're joking!"

"I wish I were. I don't want to leave this house."

"But we're not going to pay three times as much rent as our neighbors. That's ridiculous!"

"But Gordon, don't you think we should evaluate what it's worth to us? Don't you think you should consider the whole situation and see if we think the rent is something we should be willing to pay for the privilege of being in?"

"In what? A corner between the garbage dump and the brewery?"

"Don't be silly. You know what I mean."

"I don't know. Let's think it over carefully. I've got a class now, hon. See you later, okay? Don't worry about it. We'll work it out."

Don't worry about it. Don't worry that you've heard the banyan tree whispering and have only half understood what it said. Don't worry that you have glimpsed the oneness of all life and still feel divided and uncertain. Don't worry that you might have to move on with all the tight bands of fear undefined and choking you, with the world thrown open and no place to hide for safety. Don't worry about it.

That evening Tommy and Wing and the Jeng boys came over. China Pearl had stayed home to work on her new dress, and I missed her. Somehow I needed another woman's opinion in the group.

The boys sprawled on the floor and over the brown corduroy sofa, eating brownies and talking.

"What do you fellows think we should do?" Gordon asked. "Should we pay the extra rent and stay, or leave?"

"How much?" Tommy asked.

"Maybe thirty percent."

Tommy whistled and rolled his eyes.

"People in the village will know," he said. "Everybody knows everything you do."

"And they'll laugh and say you've been taken for a fool," Wing said with his typical candor.

"Thanks a lot," Gordon said. "That makes me feel great."

"Wan-Ding, looking for a sucker!" said Wing, using the expression that incorporated our Chinese name, and the whole tense group exploded with laughter.

The eldest Jeng boy was quiet, his soft face wincing for our discomfort. "I think most important," he said gently, "is that people will wonder why you stay. If you can pay such a high rent, why do you live in such a poor neighborhood as ours? You must have some strange reason, they will say, and everyone will begin to guess why."

"Perhaps the Kai-Fong will think you are Communists, come to stir up social discontent."

"And the Communists will think you are agents, working for the American CIA."

"And the other Americans will think you are trying to shame them by living more simply, to show them they do not need so many things."

"Or the Chinese will think you live here because you are sorry for them."

I listened to the swirl of voices in the room and knew none of our reasons had been dishonest, but they were too unusual to describe easily to people. Perhaps we were only learning what they were as we went along. We were even learning new definitions of honesty, only recognizing our truest reasons as we discovered them.

I looked at Tommy's face, and it had that look I had seen the night we tried to organize the youth club, a shy look of love and loyalty that had come up against an insurmountable obstacle.

"How do you feel about it?" I asked.

"Of course, we want you to stay," he said quietly.

I glanced around the room. These were our friends. For almost a year we had made no effort to cultivate others, to reach back into our own culture. These young Asians were our closest confidants, and they were telling us something I was not ready to hear.

On Saturday morning, Gordon went back to the school to finish some reports, and I went down the winding street with Mike and Chris to the vegetable market.

Lee Sang chatted as he weighed out the *choi sum*. I could see his youngest sleeping in an apple box under the counter.

"How old is Mike now?" Lee Sang asked politely.

"Eleven."

"My son is ten. Do you know of a good primary school where he could go to learn English? I know Ding Sang's school is a high school. Where does Mike go?"

"The American School."

"Ah yah, horses and devils, that's too expensive for me. How would a man like me pay so much for one child?"

"I know," I said and stopped. What good would it do to tell him that our organization paid for it, that we actually lived on very little money? In fact, how could I even pretend that I lived on the same street as Lee Sang? My options, my eventualities, were not the same. I had never thought of it on this level before, not on the level of personhood, but on the level of opportunity.

Gordon was home later that afternoon, and we discussed the problem.

"I've never had any illusions about the situation," he said, calmly. "Everyone knows we live here because we choose to. The only problem now is whether a higher rent will really separate us from the village people. If so, what is the point in staying here? Maybe we're being forced to take an honest look at the real situation."

"But I'm not ready to leave yet."

"Even if it isn't honest to stay?"

"But it was! Does honesty change?"

"Maybe the way we see it does. What seems dead serious today can seem a little funny tomorrow."

"Then what shall we do?"

"I think there are only two options," he said. "Either move back to the Western community, or live here for real."

"What do you mean, for real?"

"Rent a shop on the street, cancel our salary check from New York, make our living here, and survive like the rest of the people with no outside securities."

I looked at him and gasped. The insurance. The social security. The pension plan. The medical coverage. The check—

"The kids!" I said. "We couldn't! How could they ever go to college?"

"How will anybody on this street go to college?" he asked.

And I knew that I could not listen to him yet, that I wanted to stay on this street even if it were not honest, even if I were fooling myself . . . that I would stay here at all costs until I found what I was looking for.

But what those costs might be began slowly to dawn on me. That night we decided to take the children and go out for supper. Suddenly we were very aware of them, of the effect this decision would have on their futures.

The three older children sat in the back seat of the green Morris Oxford, and Chris sat between us in the front. It was a warm windy evening, and we drove down the highway along the sea, from the village through the Western community and on to the downtown.

"Children," Gordon began, clearing his throat. "We have something important to talk over with you. We want you to understand that the final decision will be up to your mother and me, but we want to hear your opinions on it."

"What is it?" Marita asked. "Our birthday presents?"

"No, not that. You see, we're having to make up our minds whether we're going to live in the village any longer, or if we should move closer to your school where we used to live."

There was a dead silence in the back seat. I turned around to see if they had heard. All three of them were sitting with their mouths open, speechless.

Finally there was a disbelieving croak and a giggle from Marita.

"Do you mean we have a *choice?*" she asked incredulously.

"Boy!" said Mike. "Hey!"

"What do you mean?" Deidra asked, unsure she had understood correctly.

"We mean, would you rather live in Check Wan or Shallow Water Bay?"

It was quiet again, until Marita volunteered to be the spokeswoman.

"I'll tell you how we all feel," she said. "You see, we didn't ever say anything because we knew how interested you two were in living in the village, and we really like the kids there and everything, but we can't talk to them very well like you and Mom can, and now we've stopped studying Cantonese and started learning French, and in the village everyone comes up to us and pinches us and looks in the grocery bag when you send us to buy stuff at the store, and they say I'm fat because I eat butter . . . and . . . oh, I don't know, lots of stuff. If I say too much, you'll scold me for being prejudiced and rude to Chinese people."

"No, this is one night you can say anything. No words forbidden."

"Well, you see, we like to play with the village kids, but we have a hard time explaining games or learning theirs, and well, when we bring friends home from the school, they ask us why we live where we do, and I'm afraid they'll think our parents are some kind of kooks or something. And then the village kids see the American kids coming home with us, and they call them foreign devils and run—And, I don't know. I want to be everybody's friend too, but how can you?"

"Yeah," Deidra finally chimed in, "and I get so mixed up sometimes. I walk on the street and see all the Chinese people, and I feel just right, like I was born here and I belong. And then I see other Americans walking in the village, and it makes me mad or scared or something, like I'm afraid they'll be rude to the village people, like the village people will hate me for it because I'm an American, and I feel sometimes like it's OUR village and these are OUR friends, and like we're the only foreigners who understand them, and then I know that's proud to feel that way, and I shouldn't feel that way, should I? Because it's another kind of prejudice—I mean, there are other good Americans too, aren't there?"

"But it's okay, you guys," Mike said, "if it really means a lot to you to live there, we can work it out. I don't have bad feelings about anybody, so it doesn't matter to me where I live. I really like Tommy and his brothers, and the beach and all those little shops, I really do. I think I'd miss them. I don't know. Both places are nice."

We sat in the car, driving along, listening to our brave young children trying to make a decision far too complex and involved for them, a decision that at once violated their wishes and rang true to their inborn sense of human relatedness. Why did being loyal to one group mean being disloyal to another? Why couldn't the two sides come together?

There was a resigned sigh from the back seat.

"But we'll do whatever you guys say," Marita said. "It really doesn't matter."

It really doesn't matter. It was the first apathetic statement I had ever heard Marita make in her life, and it frightened me more than all her bombastic belligerence. Things should matter. Was she already becoming afraid of losing our love, our approval, if she disagreed with our ideas about life?

I sat staring out of the window, knowing that when people choose against their deep wishes, something of life in them dies or goes dormant and becomes the seed of resentment that grows into alienation. And was not alienation within one's family even more tragic than alienation between worlds, between races. Or was it all a part of one brokenness?

Something within me whispered urgently that with our children this was a crisis point, and if we did not hear them, something would be destroyed in all of us, in the name of a good cause.

The mail came in its usual manner, with a swish and a plop under the front door. I picked up two magazines and a letter. The return address on the letter was from someone I had never heard of, and I tore it open curiously.

It was from a friend of a friend, who was coming to Hong Kong to live for a period of two years. We had known the friend in school, and the woman writing the letter had been referred to us by her. Jean and her husband Scott were being sent to Hong Kong by a major American television network. Jean would live in Hong Kong, and Scott would spend most of his time as a reporter in Vietnam, coming home once every ten weeks. They had two small children and wondered if we could recommend a place for them to live.

I looked at the date. They would be coming in a week.

Suddenly I looked around the house. It seemed bleak and bare, foot-tracked, and covered with mold.

I looked down at my faded slacks and blouse, my rubber toe-thongs. The wife of a network reporter. She would probably be dressed in silks and furs. Well, silks, at least.

I resolved to go shopping before they came. Something new to wear would do my spirits good.

In spite of the fact that it was still March, the days had grown hot. One afternoon the children begged to go swimming, and finally, to get some peace and quiet, I let them go. Ah Wai was all in a flutter about the cold water and the wrong moon, but I decided if she were that superstitious, it was her problem, not mine. The children were anxious, and I was free to go with them.

We walked through the market, dressed in swim suits and shirts, piled with inflatable tubes and mats. The shopkeepers waved and smiled at us, shaking their heads at the impatience of Americans, even Westerners who were almost like Chinese. It was considered a racial weakness of ours.

The water was too cold for me, but the children splashed and swam and had a wonderful time. Chris's nose was running, and he seemed terribly chilled after half an hour in the water, so I took him out, dried him, and told him to sit in the sun. I had noticed for a few days he had not been too well, so I wanted to be careful. When I dried him off, he sat shivering under the towel until he fell asleep with his head against me.

When the other children came out of the sea, I woke Chris. His eyes were heavy, and his body was hot. I could tell he had a fever. I picked him up and carried him with his head across my shoulder and the towel around him. He was still shivering.

By the time we got home from the beach, it was after five o'clock. I tried to call the school, but Gordon had left and was on his way home. I knew it was useless to take a bus and go to the medical clinic downtown because that too closed at five o'clock.

I laid Chris on his bed and sponged him, feeling his small body grow hotter and hotter. I finally took his temperature and saw that it was nearly 105 degrees.

I stood looking at the thermometer, and my knees started shaking.

"God," I said aloud, "what am I going to do?"

Ah Wai shuffled into the room, looking at me balefully.

"I told you, Missy, it's the wrong moon."

"Don't be ridiculous, Ah Wai," I said. "He's had this coming for several days. He didn't get it in half an hour in the water."

"It's the wrong moon to swim," she muttered, and put away a pile of wash accusatively. "Poor Tisso. We Chinese never go until the fourth moon. Maybe's he's like Chinese babies, being born here."

She came to the bed and stroked his forehead.

"There is a Chinese herb to take away fever," she said. "Shall I go to the herb shop and get some for you?"

If it had been myself, I would have tried it. But to feed Chris some unknown drug in a time of sickness was more than I could do.

"Not yet," I said. "I think Ding Sang should be home in a minute."

I closed the door when she shuffled out and sponged Chris's hot body. His muscles were tight, and I was terrified that he would go into a convulsion from the fever. Already small jerks were twitching his little limbs.

"Oh God," I said an incoherent mixture of prayer, anger, and tears. "Where is that Gordon? What am I supposed to do? What *is* there to do?"

Mike opened the door and tiptoed in.

"Wing is here," he said.

"Tell him I'll see him later," I said, tight-lipped.

"What?" Mike was big-eyed.

Wing was standing in the door behind Mike.

"Ding Tai," he said politely. "What is the matter?"

"Chris—"

"You must take him to the doctor."

"The clinic downtown is closed."

"Where's Ding Sang?"

"I don't know. He should have been home over an hour ago. I don't know where he is."

Wing bent over the bed and touched Chris with a kindly hand.

"There is a doctor," he said. "The fisher people go to a doctor down by the other beach. He practices Western medicine. They say he's a good man, that he only charges a dollar or maybe some fresh fish for taking care of them."

"Do you know where this man is?"

"Haih. I know. Do you want me to show you?"

"Anything. I've got to do something."

I picked up the small, limp child and wrapped him in a light blanket. I held him close to me as we walked through the market, his heart pounding in rapid flutters against me. People called to me, but I ran on, not even answering. My eyes were full of tears, and my throat was tight. All the ideas of the street had forsaken me. Chris was sick, and nothing else mattered.

We crossed the highway and passed the bus stop, then plunged into a thick grove of trees. It was beginning to get dark, and the shadows of the woods seemed eerie and frightful with the feverish child clasped against me. On through the woods, along a stretch of sandy beach, and finally into a tangle of houses, fences, and courtyards. I followed Wing through a gateway and into a small yard where he knocked on a door.

A woman in a flowered sam-fu came out and eyed me suspiciously. She obviously did not expect me to understand Chinese.

"Why did you bring this thing here?" she asked Wing, jutting her chin at me. "Don't you know you could cause us trouble?"

"The child is sick," Wing said simply.

It was no time for games.

"M'goi, ho m'goi nei," I begged her in her language. "Please let the doctor see him. I'll pay anything."

The woman stared at me, as if the wrong voice had come from the wrong face, smiled, and opened the door.

"What the devil," she said still speaking to Wing. "What is this person?"

"She speaks," said Wing. "Watch what you say."

I sat in the waiting room with several black-clad fisherwomen, and at long last a Chinese man came out. His hands smelled of medicines, and his American accent was unmistakable. He looked at me suspiciously.

"What's the problem with the boy?" he asked.

"A high fever. Please can you do something?"

"Who are you?"

"His mother."

He hesitated a moment then took Chris from my arms. He carried him into another room, laid him out on a table, felt his pulse, and took his temperature. Then he prepared an injection.

I stood watching him, my heart thundering in my chest. How did I know he was a real doctor? How did I know the needle was clean, that the medicine would help him and not harm him? Chris.

I watched the needle plunge in and the small muscles jump, then relax. It was done.

The Chinese man handed me a bottle of medicine.

"His fever should begin to go down in twenty minutes or so," he said in an American accent. "Give him this every four hours. I think it's just one of those sudden fevers kids get, but you'd better take him downtown to your regular doctor in the morning."

I fumbled in my pocket, but there was no money. I was not used to paying doctor bills on the spot and certainly not used to paying for them in fresh fish.

"I'm sorry, " I said apologetically, "uh, could you send me your bill?"

The man looked at me. Over his shoulder the woman in the sam-fu hovered.

"You'd better tell her," said the woman.

"This is a favor I must ask of you, now that I've done you one," he said. "You cannot tell anyone you've been here, or you will cause me to go to jail. I take care of the fisherfolk, and what I do for them is my own business. But if I charge a foreigner, I can be sued because I don't have my license yet. I am a licensed doctor in your country, but the British license is different. So you see, I have risked my neck to help you."

"You can count on it," I said, extending my hand. "I won't cause you any trouble."

They let us out of the locked doorway, and I saw a woman come in with a basketful of fish. We walked back along the beach and through the woods, across the road and into the market. We were almost home when I heard the toot of Gordon's horn beside us on the street.

"Where have you been?" I asked. "I needed help. Where in thunder were you?"

"Don't you remember I told you I'd be later tonight, that I'd stop and look around on my way home at a few places for Jean and Scott? But what happened, is somebody hurt?"

I climbed into the car and told Gordon what had happened.

"You took a chance," he said.

"You do, when you're desperate. When it's a matter of life and death, you trust people. What else can you do?"

"Life and death?" he quizzed me. "A kid's fever, life and death?"

I sat in the car, feeling foolish, wondering why I had reacted so violently. Was it the undefined sense of vulnerability to disaster, the feeling that life could hurt and I had no recourse?

The beginning of the next week I took the checkbook and went downtown on the bus. I went to a British department store and tried on clothes, taking a long hard look at myself in the mirror. I was thin enough, almost gaunt. My hair had been cropped short for convenience sake, and I looked like a prime case of self-denial for a cause. I decided to remedy the situation.

I bought a smart black pants suit, a pair of sandals with high heels, a bikini, and a long straight wig. I got on the bumpy bus for Check Wan feeling like I had my queendom in a plastic bag.

Gordon's reaction was enthusiastic, if a little shaken. A few nights later we went out to dinner together, pants suit, wig, and sandals.

It was dark by the wine factory when we walked to the car with only the street light casting an uncertain bug-filled glow on the corner. Gordon went around to open the car door for me, properly escorting this new lady-friend of his.

Two boys were sitting on the railing by the sea.

"Who is that with Ding Sang?" one asked quietly.

"I don't know," said the other. "It's not Ding Tai. She's not that stylish."

"Ah yah," said the other. "Ding Sang must have a new woman."

We climbed in the car, laughing quietly, but the laughter stung.

"Do you ever get bored with me?" I asked.

"Of course not," he said gallantly, looking at the strange apparition beside him. I sat under the wig, feeling that I had changed the outside of me, but inside things were still in the same state of confusion.

The next night, all the confrontation we had been avoiding came at once. It was after supper, and the March wind sweeping through the village streets carrying a hundred fragrances tempted us to go out and take a walk through the shops. The children preferred to stay in and watch a television show, and Gordon and I walked alone. We walked past Yau Tai, busily sorting out her day's leftover produce, smiling as ever, with her troubles and her children all around her. We waved to the mother of the crippled child and met the father, a soft-spoken man with a kind face, not the hairy ogre I had envisioned him to be. We passed the Jengs, eating their evening meal in the shop around the card table and wandered on to the snake wine shop.

Gordon paused in front of the shop, gazing at the mottled coils entwined in the huge glass jars. He turned to me.

"How would you like a sip of snake wine?" he asked mischievously.

I shivered.

"Not that. Anything but that!"

"C'mon. Let's go in!"

"I don't want to!"

"C'mon. You're not afraid, are you?" "No, it just turns my stomach!"

We went in, at his insistence. All year I had passed the snake wine shop, imagining it to be a weird, mysterious place where vipers hissed and the floor was covered with reptiles. But when we walked inside, I was surprised to find it a rather ordinary shop, run by two grey-haired ladies with placid faces. They showed us the various types of snake wine: one to brace against the cold, one to improve circulation, and one to improve male potency.

The kind-faced lady poured a tiny glass full and offered it to us.

I wanted to bolt for the door. All my openness and belief in the oneness of all things could not cover the revulsion I felt. I shook my head, glad that the lady was not Jeng Tai or anyone I knew well, that the insult would not be personal.

"I—I can't," I gulped.

"No, thank you," Gordon smiled at the lady. "Maybe we'll come back another time when we're more used to the idea. My wife is afraid of snakes."

We went out the door, and Gordon caught my hand, laughing.

"It's all in the way you think of it," he said. "Just imagine they're pickled herring or something Dutch."

"Don't ever get me in there again," I sputtered. "That stuff looks positively *evil*."

"What happened to my open, accepting wife?" he smiled.

I did not know. It had been an extraordinarily rough week.

Deidra was not watching television when we came back to the house. The sound of a child's record player came from the girls' bedroom, playing the new record she had asked for on her tenth birthday.

I went up the stairs to the white room, ready to flop across the bed and think things through. The matter of the eviction was hanging over us and needed to be discussed. Time was moving on, and a decision must be reached. What would I do if Gordon demanded I sacrifice the ideals that had come to mean so much?

On the pillow was a note, scribbled in Deidra's schoolgirl handwriting. Notes had become the favorite vehicle for saying things too difficult to express aloud.

I absorbed the message, the feeling of guilt and confusion deepening:

Bridge over Troubled Water is a nice record, but when it says, IF YOU NEED A FRIEND, how can the record help you? If you really need a friend, a friend won't pop out of the record. The Bridge over Troubled Water is USELESS.

Attached to it was another scrap of paper:

On the other hand, I'm glad I have the record. When your best friend didn't want to come home with you after school because your street stinks, and your second best friend is spending the night at someone else's house, and you're feeling small, it's nice to know that great guys like Simon and Garfunkel have gone through feeling weird, helpless, and unwanted. It's nice to know you aren't *that* weird.

Love, DeDe.

I covered my face and began to cry. What was happening? Did a ten-year-old really have feelings like that?

When Gordon came upstairs, he read the note.

"How are you going to handle that?" he asked.

I knew he was going to say that I had been wrong all along, that we were over our heads. It made me defensive.

"You can't always listen to kids either," I argued. "It's like the day they wanted to go swimming. They would have been furious if I hadn't taken them, and yet when Chris got sick, it was *my* fault for letting him get chilled. I think we have to make a decision as adults and not be pressured by the kids. My parents never listened to me."

"But you should at least go talk to her."

"I know."

I went downstairs and found Deidra alone in her room, listening to the record, her dark eyes round and wounded like some remembered ghost of my own childhood.

"It'll be okay," I said, hugging her. "Don't worry. Dad and I will get it all figured out."

"When?" was all she said.

When the children were in bed, we both knew it was the night to talk it out to the bitter end. There were only two more weeks left in March, and a decision must be made by the first of April.

"I don't see what there is to discuss," Gordon began. "It's been great here, but it's over. I don't feel like pouring all that extra money into a house like this. We could be much more comfortable for the price somewhere else."

"But who wants to be comfortable?" I said. "That really isn't the point. Maybe if we did pay the extra for the privilege of living here, it would show the villagers we really do feel a part of them, really do love them as persons."

"I think you're rationalizing. The people here are too practical for that. All the extra money would do is cut us off from everyone we know. You heard the boys yourself, listing all the questions that would be asked."

"But I think we should be able to overcome those suspicions."

"It's not worth it."

"Not worth it . . . *not worth it* . . . how do you think you can measure the worth of everything in dollars and cents? My God, you haven't learned a thing here! You're still counting penny for penny what's *worth* it! How can you measure an experience like this in dollars and cents?"

"Somebody has to think about finances."

"It's not just finances. You always seem to be so bound up in what we *should* do. I'm so sick of hearing the word SHOULD. You haven't got a shred of imagination anymore! You're losing your guts! You're getting tight and stingy and stiff, and just when I'm trying to figure out what it means to be a free person, you're running the other way."

He blinked and looked straight at me as if I had hit him, a tide of indignation rising in his eyes.

"You ought to be glad I'm a responsible person," he said. "Would you really like it if I just let go, if I lived without any restraints, without any sense of responsibility to you or the kids. Would you like that?"

The note, the snake wine, the fever, the eviction notice, the unsolved questions. They all churned in my head, making a mad confusion. I was pinned under them, frightened, ready to be a part of the village wholeness yet shattered into a thousand fragments.

"Do what you want!" I said angrily. "But just get off my back! I'm sick of your tightness, your stiffness!"

It was the first night I could remember falling asleep without speaking to each other. I, half-asleep, heard the crash of the sea on the shore below and the hundred night sounds. The sea was around me, a huge pool of life, and I was bobbing on the surface, ready to sink, a tiny helpless speck in a great swirling force.

Deeper, deeper into sleep, down into the areas of fear that lay buried in my mind, the helplessness, the unconscious.

I was walking on the street and saw a lovely Chinese girl, dressed in pink, pushing a pig cart. She pushed the cart through our front door and parked it in the living room. On the cart sat the Eurasian child, blinking innocently at me with his yellow-green eyes.

I ran out the door and called for Gordon, but he was nowhere to be found. I roamed the streets, burning with a fever, until I came to the wine factory. It was almost more than I could bear to make myself look inside, but when I did, I could see it clearly—the shiny eyes standing out in the darkness of the stone building. And as I stared at it, I knew I was coming face to face with the ghost of the wine factory, the ghost of my own fears of destruction and loss. As I stared, horrified, I saw the ghost taking form. The green eyes were suddenly surrounded by a body. It was Gordon, standing in the wine factory, taking a shower.

"Come on," I tried to shout to him, but my voice was a squeak, "come on—someone has a pig-cart in our living room, some girl with a Eurasian child—come and get them out!"

But he only stretched his limbs and soaped himself and looked at me disinterestedly. "I might as well tell you," he said, "that's my child."

I felt sick, a shock went through my body.

"*I thought you said you weren't like that,*" I said, "*that you cared for us, that you had standards and were responsible.*"

"*Awww, now you know I'm not, so what?*" said the languid voice. "*I've fathered three children outside the family.*"

I stood looking at the face that was not quite Gordon, a vacuous face like that of a male centerfold with no person inside, and a tide of anger rose inside me, an anger strong enough to kill.

I half awoke and felt him sleeping beside me. In anger I raised my fist and came smashing down on his shoulder.

"You!" I screamed. "Why didn't you tell me? Why did you trick me?"

He sat up, fending off the blows, suddenly startled awake.

"What in the world are you doing?" he asked sleepily. "What did I do? What's the matter?"

I was awake and feeling foolish, striking out at him for something I had dreamed.

I told him the dream, feeling a confessional sense of relief. He sighed and laughed a tired laugh.

"What would make you dream that?" he asked. "You know I'd never do anything like that. If anything, I'm too stiff and respectable for you—no sense of imagination."

"Whew! I've decided you could be a lot worse."

"But what would make you dream that? You're not worried about me are you? Have I done something?"

"No," I admitted, "I think it goes deeper than the relationship between the two of us. It's a kind of basic helplessness I feel, like I'm lost in something big and there's no way I can control life. I feel that something is going to hurt me, destroy me."

"Don't you believe in me?" he asked, now fully awake.

"I think it's even worse than that. I think I don't believe in myself. Everyone seems stronger than I, and I have this fear that anyone, even you, could hurt me."

"You could hurt me just as much."

"Women don't hurt men. It's always men who hurt women."

"That's not true. If you got all hung up on living here and walked out on me and the children because I felt we had to move, that would hurt me, hurt all of us, wouldn't it?"

"But it's usually the men who hurt women."

"Women can do it, too, especially somebody like you with a wild imagination. You scare me to death sometimes."

"Me?"

"Yes, you!"

I lay in the darkness, with the current of fear suddenly reversed. "*I* scare *you?*"

"You bet you do."

I lay quietly, overcome with the novelty of the idea. From somewhere in the darkness of the room, it began to pour into me. The balance, the wholeness, the understanding that I was not the good and innocent at the mercy of evil. In me, there was the power to hurt and destroy as well as to love and create. I should accept this evil and claim responsibility for it, if ever there was to be safety in this new vastness that was God. Far from being depressed, I felt a strange power from knowing that I too was evil as well as good, that I was not defenseless.

And then from the opposite side of the darkness rushed the knowledge that I was good as well as evil, that I would choose *not* to use my power to destroy, that I was equipped with good and evil to use responsibly, to use knowingly, to use creatively. I was love and hate, light and darkness, strength and gentleness. I was all that was. It was no longer outside me, ready to crush my emptiness with its power, but the power was inside me, equal to the pressure. Stabilized. The good and evil had washed together in me, and the fear was gone. In its place flooded an enormous peace, a blending, a calm.

I reached out to Gordon, a sense of wonder filling me.

"Do you know what?" I asked. "Something has just happened to me. I don't know how it happened, but suddenly I'm not afraid. Suddenly, I'm free to believe in you because I believe in myself. I don't think you could ever do anything that could make me hate you now because I don't need the right actions from you to keep me from being afraid. Does that make sense to you?"

"Go on," he said, "I'm getting it."

"You've probably got it already, you're so calm," I said. "But all of a sudden I know what it means to be whole, a good-bad person, complete in myself. I don't feel like you have to fill up the emptiness or calm my fears. I understand only God can fill me, then I've got something to share with you. I feel so strong, so beautiful!"

It was a strange moment to cry, but they were tears of triumph. I had found it.

The sea that had sounded angry a few hours before sounded peaceful now, and we lay quietly, knowing that from this point everything would work out. Nothing seemed impossible, not even a sip of snake wine. After one has discovered the snake in Eden and eaten him, what is a little sip of wine?

the other side
of the mountain

In the village, spring had come almost imperceptibly. With the island's semitropical climate, nothing had completely died during the winter, and the resurgence of life came about so silently, it was merely an affirmation carried on the wind, a whisper that said, *yes, life will go on.*

I wandered through the market, feeling the resurgence around me and within me. Everywhere in pots and vases, there were clumps of downy white pussy willows for sale in preparation for Ching Ming. I bought a small bunch to take home and strolled down the street, inhaling the warm revitalizing breath of the wind, feeling thawed from the winter of fear and struggle, and anxious to feel the warmth of summer. Somehow since the night of the violent dream and the discussion with Gordon, I felt curiously free, loose-jointed, uninhibited. The black pants suit, which had been the symbol of daring a short while ago, already seemed wintry and stodgy and had been replaced with a bright yellow paisley; now I strode along the street, every part of my body alive and moving. It was spring, and all the dark winters were being left behind.

In the house on the corner, Ah Wai found a vase for the pussy willows. I noticed that she had a sprig pinned onto her sam-fu and asked her why.

"It is for new life," she said. "At Ching Ming, when we go to visit the graves and think about the dead, how can one bear to think of life that has ended without thinking of life that goes on? We think of death in the springtime when all around us life is coming new again. How else could one bear it?"

"Do you think of people living again?" I asked.

She gave me that here-comes-the-stork-again look.

"Nothing ever completely dies," she said patiently, "and all people live on in their children. But why would anyone want to live himself again? Ah yah, if I get through this once, I'll be doing well."

Outside the window a scissors-sharp voice rose up like a summer locust.

"Mai hung mei a Mai hung mei a—"

I glanced out the window and saw an old man sitting on the sidewalk selling fragrant sticks of sandalwood to be burned at the temple, or in homes, or on graves. I breathed in the strange fragrance on the spring wind and felt an admixture of living and dying that was so harmonious it seemed to be one statement.

There was a knock and a gust of dusty wind, and Tong stood at the front door. Under his arm was a pack of paintings. He seemed more radiant than ever this morning, bronzed and shining like a happy Buddha, with the smell of the sun and the wind on his clothes.

"Wai, Tong! Where have you been hiding?"

"Painting," he smiled. "An artist must hide, or all his thoughts are stolen in the busyness of people."

"What have you done?"

"Ah, I got the very good news. You remember you said, 'Make the boats broad?'"

"I do. Did you make me a painting of the boats?"

"No, I didn't bring it here. That's the good news. After you told me, 'Don't let other peoples change you, make the boats like they feel good,' I did that. And the day I take it to my boss, the Anglissman, he had this friend to dinner. And the friend saw my boats. 'Ah, I like it,' he said. And the Anglissman said, 'Tong, I said you must not make the boats so fat.' But his friend put up his hand and said, 'No, I like the boats so fat like that, they look strong.' And then he said, 'I will show you how much I like the boats.' And he took out his money and gave me a hundred dollars. A hundred dollars! He bought my picture!"

"Ayie, Tong! Congratulations!" I put out my hand and clasped his, and we shook hands until we were practically doing a dance. "Ayie! That's wonderful! I wish I could have seen it!"

"This is especially wonderful because this man is in, what you call it, Mai go bou?"

"Advertising?"

"Haih. This my picture of the boats, he will make many copies to go on a calendar. Twelve different artists in Hong Kong will have paintings on this, one for each month, and I will be one."

"You should never have let him change your work."

"Ah, but it was *his* friend. I still am in debt to him."

And I saw in his carved face a mixture of life and death, of joy and sorrow, of freedom and bondage. And outside the voice of the old man rose up like a summer locust, selling fragrant sticks to be burned on graves.

Tong was silent for a moment, listening to the voice outside the window.

"I hear you may be leaving the village," he said. "The boys told me you asked them what to do. I was busy that night at the Anglissman's house."

"How would you have advised us?"

Tong was quiet, sitting like an immobile statue for a full minute. Thoughts seemed to be arising out of a deep well inside him, reaching his throat, his face, and finally his mouth.

"Many times I sit on the hillside looking out over the sea," he said, "and thoughts come to me. It seems that my life is always going up and down, fighting my way up the mountain, climbing the slippery places, falling on the rocks, sliding back, and then one day I get to the top of the mountain. When I get there, to the top of the mountain, I feel good. I can sit down and see everywhere. It all seems so simple. I can see everywhere, but I am far from everything. I can't reach out with my hand and touch the valley I came from, and I do not know what there is down the other side of the mountain."

I waited as he shifted his position, listening for his words.

"I have been watching you, you and Ding Sang, watching you climb this mountain of living in a way which is strange to you. And every time I have seen you before, you were still climbing. But now, this morning, what is it? There is a different *gam gok,* a different feeling on your face. Have you come to the top of the mountain?"

"I think so," I said softly.

"And do you want to go backward or forward?"

"Always forward."

"Then you must go down the other side of the mountain and see what is there."

I searched Tong's face and knew he was a poet as well as an artist, and I loved him for all that he was and all that he was not.

It was a solemn time in the village. Tong went with his mother to sweep the grave of his father, who had been dead almost twenty years. The mother, like a good Chinese widow, had never remarried and went regularly to commune with the spirit of her deceased husband. The children of the village took the occasion as one more festival and enjoyed the prospect of a picnic, games of jump rope and tumbling, and a hike to a high place. As usual, the occasion was observed by each participant at the level of his own life-experience, and none forced the other to share his sorrow or his joy.

For several days I pondered the practical meaning of Tong's word-picture, *the other side of the mountain.* Where did the path lead down the other side of the mountain?

One morning I began to find the path. I was at Mr. Lee's vegetable stand, buying a supply of fresh greens, when I saw a Western woman struggling along the street with two small children and a load of groceries. One child was crying because his mother did not have an extra hand, and he clung to her skirt making it impossible for the woman to walk, which caused her to scold him, frightening him even more.

My first response was, *these Western women who treat their children so cruelly. It's no wonder they grow up to produce weapons and become a menace to the earth.*

And then I felt my thoughts reverse. What would I do if this woman were Chinese? Would I not reach out and say, *"May I help you?"*

I felt the rusty hinges of my mind opening, the other side of it that had lain dormant for a year, and I suddenly wondered what would happen if I treated this foreigner with the same openness, the same freedom and love that I had extended to the Chinese people of the village? The idea seemed exciting.

I came up beside her.

"It looks like you have your hands full," I said. "May I help you?"

She swung around, a bit shocked, to see if she should know me from somewhere. Obviously she did not.

"Oh, thank you," she said. "If you could take this one's hand until we get out of this traffic. My car's just around the corner."

"Do you live here?" I asked, taking the crying child.

"Oh Heavens no! We've just been in Hong Kong a few months, and I don't think I'll ever get used to it. Everything is so strange. Where do you live?"

"Right down the street. That's our house on the corner. Would you like to stop in for a drink and rest a minute?"

"Why . . . I . . . I mean you're very kind. I don't even know your name. Why are you inviting me in for a drink?"

"Why not?" I laughed.

She came in and we talked, and her children played with Chris. It was, surprisingly, just as adventurous as having tea with Wong Tai. This stranger was a person full of thoughts and ideas about life, a person no less exciting because she had come from my own country and from my own cultural roots.

And I began to see the dim outline of the path down the other side of the mountain.

Just before lunch I went to the store to buy extra food, a cake mix and Western supplies that I did not ordinarily buy. Jean and Scott would be arriving that afternoon and were coming home with Gordon for dinner. Shallow Water Bay lay between the school and the village, and it would be convenient for him to pick them up from their hotel on the way home.

When I went into the Store, Hong Sang looked up and smiled.

"Good morning," I said, "how's your little girl doing?"

He patted the head of the frail child beside him.

"Not too well. A few days ago she had to have blood, and the doctor says she may need more. I gave some blood already. It's hard for us Chinese to give blood. We are thinner and weaker, not so strong as you Siyan."

A thought crossed my mind and then died in midair.

"I'd give some blood for her," I said, "but they won't take mine. I had hepatitis a few years ago, and there might be a danger."

He nodded, his face a curious pale shade, as though he were suffering for his child.

I prepared the dinner, excited at the thought of Jean and Scott and their children coming. A few weeks ago, their coming had seemed threatening, like the outside intruding into our experiment. Now I found myself humming and smiling while I worked in the kitchen. I wondered what Jean would be like. I had discarded the silks-and-furs idea after thinking of traveling with two small children. I wondered what Scott would be like, a real live television reporter, a somebody in my own cultural system. The thought was almost overwhelming.

They came to the door with Gordon, four tired travelers. Jean looked smart in her beige suit and sunglasses, but a bit worn at the edges by the red-haired baby in her arms. Scott came in, big, athletic, blond, and blue-eyed, with a three-year-old daughter in his arms. When I saw them, a terrible rush of nostalgia came over me for everything I thought I had forgotten. I greeted them with all my caution and hesitancy gone, in a glad rush of new beginnings of old things.

We ate together, talking of things and people we knew. They looked around our house by the sea, marveling at its uniqueness.

"This is a neat little pad you've got here," Scott said in his booming announcer's voice. "Could you find something like this for us?"

I saw the hesitation flash in Jean's eyes, the same kind of hesitation I had felt when we came to the village. She turned to me.

"Would you recommend living here in the village?" she asked. "I mean, for us?"

I glanced at her, new from the protected shelter of the United States, without the knowledge of a word of Chinese, with two small children and a husband who would be gone ten weeks at a time. What had been heaven for me might be hell for her.

"I don't know," I said slowly. "Why don't you see if there's something in the American community?"

"What're you trying to do," Scott teased, "be exclusive? I'm going to be slogging through the mud in Vietnam, and Jeanie might just like it here. It would toughen her up!"

"And I just might not like it here," she said, reading my glance.

"How much longer are you living here?" Scott asked.

Gordon and I looked at each other.

"We have to decide that by next week," he said. "I showed Jean and Scott the place in Shallow Water Bay on the way out. It's an upstairs flat with a garden and a downstairs flat that opens up by the end of the month, for not much more than we'd pay for staying here."

That night when they had gone back to the hotel, I sat out on the balcony, listening to the sound of the sea. It was the same sea that washed the beach in Shallow Water Bay, but here it seemed different. Here it was the mirror of the morning sky, the traffic way of boatmen singing and calling and splashing nets. At night it was a starry curtain hung low, with twinkling lights of fishing boats creeping in to the shore like stars that had lost the line between earth and sky. Where else would the sea ever have the power to bewitch as it had in this village? Where else could one live so close to the bare nerve center of life? Where else was there to *live*?

Tommy came to the door the next morning, and I sat down to chat with him. He was obviously troubled about something, but I knew it was useless to ask him directly. It always required several cups of tea before anyone in the village could come to the point about a serious matter.

He began talking about his after school job as messenger at the bank, the humiliation of wearing a white uniform and being looked down on by his friends, the struggle of coming home from a full day of work and study and then trying to be older brother and father in the household, and of his fear of failing the important English examination to be taken in a few weeks.

Having talked himself out, he sat quietly for a few moments, staring at the floor.

"I always wonder," he said thoughtfully, "if you can't believe in the gods, how do you know what is true?"

"Doesn't your heart tell you?" I asked.

"Ayie, but my heart changes so often. Today this is true, and tomorrow that is true. I feel afraid. Maybe there are gods who could guide me, but all I have seen of such things seems like ignorance and superstition. The gods leave people to make mistakes, to suffer, to go hungry and die, to kill each other. How could I believe in such useless gods?"

I moved around the edges of his fear carefully, still wounded from my own struggles with the mysteries of life.

"Did you learn in school about the one God, the Creator-God who was the beginning?"

"Haih. And before that I learned how the world was made according to the Chinese legend. My mind has been filled with two beginnings that makes me wonder if either of them is true or if I could as easily make up my own."

I had never heard the Chinese story of the world's beginning, and I asked him to tell it to me. His face seemed to brighten, to lose its troubled lostness in recounting the familiar in his own language.

"In the beginning, there was a Great Power, and this power was male and female. The male and female divided into the Yin and the Yang, and then from the Yin and the Yang came the lesser and the greater. These four powers made one person named Poon Giht, or sometimes called Pan Ku. This Pan Ku had a job to do, and this was to take the huge blocks of stone floating through space and hew the earth and sky out of them. He took a hammer and a chisel, and carved out the sun, moon, and stars; then he turned to the earth where four animals helped him: the dragon, the turtle, the tiger, and the phoenix.

"For eighteen thousand years he worked to make the earth, and to be big enough to do his work, he grew six feet every day.

"Then when his work was finished, he lay down and the life went out of him and into the world he had made, bringing the whole world alive. His head filled the mountains with life, and his breath became the wind. His voice gave power to the thunder. His left eye gave light to the sun, and his right eye lighted the moon. His white beard lighted the scattered dust of the stars, and his limbs stretched over the four corners of the East, West, North and South. His body became the five sacred mountains, and his blood flowed in the rivers. Veins and muscles became the layers of the earth, and his skin the soil. From his skin sprouted the fields and forests, and his teeth and bones made the minerals. His marrow became precious gems, and his sweat watered the crops."

"And how about humankind, people?"

"They sprang from his body too. All the life came from one source."

I looked at his troubled dark eyes and felt a deep empathy. His childhood ways had been questioned, and the ways of the West seemed equally arbitrary. How could one know what was true? What could I say to this young brother?

When I spoke, it was finding a path for myself as well.

"Tommy, you taught me something, something that I am just beginning to understand."

"I taught you?"

"Do you remember the day of the Devil Festival when you laughed and said, 'I believe in myself?'"

"Haih, but life seemed easier then."

"But, Tommy, you must remember you said that. When God breathed his breath into humankind, they lived. Your legend says that in one way, the story of the Creator-God in another. But the important thing to understand right now is that life of God in you, Tommy. And when you can believe in yourself, it is believing in part of God—the part of God that has been given to you to live. It doesn't matter if that life is hidden under a messenger's uniform or looked down on by others. You stand tall and breathe deep, Tommy, remember that the breath of God is in you!"

I saw Tommy's black eyes glisten, and his shoulders straighten, and I felt my heart pounding, carrying a new aliveness, recognizing my own origins. The words had come from somewhere, forming as I said them. They were as new to me as they were to Tommy.

I clasped his hand as he left and saw new courage in his eyes, and they reflected courage back to mine.

That evening Gordon and I took the children to the beach to walk along the sea and hunt for shells. In all the uncertainty, we seemed to be reaching for each other. Even the children seemed to sense the questions in the air, and they seemed less distant, less put upon, more hopeful, even younger.

We strolled along the seaside, Gordon and I with clasped hands while the children scampered ahead. Mike came running back with a perfectly shaped shell and gave it to me. I hugged him and he was off, and Gordon and I smiled at each other, the salt spray stinging our lips.

I thought about truth, and how our perception of it grows and changes, and how people at one time thought the world was flat and shouted heretic at those who wondered if it were round, and how they shuddered at the thought of falling off the edge, and how there are no edges any more, except in our minds.

Words began to come, and I found a piece of paper in my pocket, and borrowed Gordon's pen. They were words that seemed to be directed toward a power, an untamable force that arose in me speaking for itself.

> *If you restrict me to the depth*
> *And width and breadth of your today,*
> *Tomorrow you may feel a guilt*
> *A need to leave me far behind*
> *To occupy nostalgic shells*
> *That yesterday had housed your mind.*

I gave it to Gordon, and we read it silently, looking out over the sea and knowing what it meant.

Tommy and Wing met us in the street on the way back. Wing's face was serious.

"Hong Sang's little girl just went to the hospital," he said. "She was vomiting blood."

"Which hospital?" Gordon asked.

"The government hospital."

"Ah yah," I said, looking at the children. What would I do if one of them were vomiting blood?

"Can anything be done?" Gordon asked.

"They'll have to see," Wing said. "They're going to try to give her more blood, but they're not sure if she can take it."

"They need someone else to give to the blood bank," Tommy said. "Her father and mother have given all they can."

"What about the other relatives?"

"Ah yah," said Wing, turning a strange color. "We Chinese are afraid to give blood. It's not so easy for us. I would fight to the death before I gave anybody my blood. Ah yah, it scares me to death to think of it!"

We were uneasy about the Hong child that evening, but not knowing what to do, we waited for further word. The next day was Sunday, Easter Sunday, and my mind was taken up with laying out the children's clothes for church.

Easter morning dawned bright and sunny, and we piled into the square green car and chugged over the mountain to the Western community. As we rode along, an absurd rhyme kept running through my mind:

> The bear went over the mountain, the bear went over the mountain
> The bear went over the mountain, to see what he could see,
> The other side of the mountain, the other side of the mountain,
> The other side of the mountain, was all that he could see.

We started the long descent into Shallow Water Bay, and I gazed over the white line of beach and the towering apartment buildings. Would it be that simple? Coming down the hill, I wondered how much of the meaning discovered in the village had actually been perceived by us because of our own Christian cultural roots, how much of what we had been and known we were reading into the village situation. Could it be that our education and background had made the village more significant to us than if we had simply been there forever? Perhaps we should give credit where credit was due.

The church was full, as churches always are on Easter Sunday, with Western people and a few Asians dressed in new and beautiful clothes, bright and colorful like on the Chinese New Year Day. The wind blew up from the sea below and wrapped the church in a blanket of life and newness, the church with its symbols of death and its struggle to celebrate life. I thought of our friends in the village wearing a sprig of pussy willow while they swept the graves of their ancestors, and the Christian church singing of new life in the shadow of the cross; I knew that in mankind there is the necessity to cope with the fear of death, that to cope, one must be assured of life, of ongoing life that in some way transcends the visible end.

And that day I came to terms with the cross, not only as a death symbol, but as a life symbol. I thought of the hillside at Chinese New Year, of the poverty and stench, of the vast human potential of those sons and daughters of God almighty, and I felt the pain Christ must have felt as he looked over the world painfully aware of both mankind's potential and degradation. I looked up at the cross, with its roots in the ground, in the worst the world could offer, and its arms stretched toward the sky, reaching for our birthright, and the tears of recognition coursed down my face. This cross. My life symbol.

After the service we stood outside the church, looking over the beautiful panorama of mountains and sea. Jean and Scott were there and other travelers who had stopped in for the special day. Among them was a tall black man, traveling around the world for an international religious organization.

We began to chat with this man. There was an understanding in his eyes that helped us talk, that eventually drew out of us what was troubling us most deeply. Somehow we felt that we had suffered what he had suffered, for different reasons.

"What do you mean, living in the village is a problem?" he said. "Those are the most beautiful people in the world."

"We know that," I agreed, "but that's the problem. We might have to move. It's not fair."

He listened to the complications of our situation with his head cocked to one side, his face full of a mocking bittersweetness.

He said softly, "You guys don't know who you are, do you? Born to power and privilege, born with the equipment in your hands to change the world, and you go to a village like that and hole up because you feel guilty and ashamed for what's going on in the world. You try to hide yourselves and pretend like you're somebody else so the pressure will be off you, so you won't have to sit with the guilt on your shoulders." He suddenly exploded, "You people are part of the power system! If you've learned anything from those villagers, get back where you belong and fight your own kind! They're the ones who need you! For God's sake, don't hang on to somebody else's identity for a cover. Be yourselves, *if you dare*. People like you are a drag on society!"

We left the church feeling shaken and a little angry. The children trailed behind us, big-eyed.

"Why was he so mad?" Marita asked. "What did we do to him?"

I thought about that as we drove back over the mountain to the village.

Tommy was tending his mother's vegetable stall as we drove into the market. He waved for us to stop.

"The little Hong girl is very sick. They're not sure she'll live," he said, leaning on the window.

Gordon looked grave, and the children were silent.

"Maybe I'd better go see what I can do, if anything," he said. Tommy waved us on, and Gordon drove grimly under the banyan tree and parked the car in front of the house. We stepped over and around the step-sitters, and Gordon made his way to the telephone.

"What are you going to do?" I asked.

He dialed the hotel where Jean and Scott were staying.

"You can't give blood, can you?" he said, waiting for the phone to be answered.

"No. I—"

"Hello," he said, "Scott? This is Gordon. Listen, this is a funny thing to ask you the minute you arrive in Hong Kong, but do you mind giving some blood?"

There was a silence, and a laugh on the other end of the wire.

"Yeah, it's an emergency."

More silence.

"Okay. I'll pick you up in about twenty minutes."

He put the receiver down, gave me a quick kiss, and headed for the door. "I don't know if it will do any good, but we'll offer," he said as he disappeared.

I listened to the car motor start, wishing I could go and knowing my children were hungry for lunch.

Life goes on in the presence of death.

I prepared the food, answering their questions and feeling a strange sensation spread over me. The Chinese saying, the ancient law of the jungle, pounded through my mind, forcing itself into my consciousness.

Blood can only be repaid with blood.

Why was I thinking that?

I went upstairs, my hands still smelling of tuna fish, and looked for it in the pile of old magazines, the December issue with the bloody pictures, and stood staring at it—the photographs of bleeding children, children with Asian faces, soldiers with Western uniforms.

And I thought of them, two strong Western men holding out their arms to have a pint of blood taken, blood which might save the life of an Asian child.

And staring at the picture, I thought of the huge legendary Chinese creator who had infused the earth with his life, whose blood became the rivers, and of the life stream, the bloodstream of all people, and how significant it is that blood from one person can flow in another's veins, bringing equal life.

Blood for blood. Why had I always shivered at blood as a death symbol? It is also a life carrier. The cup of communion that had made me shiver as a death cup was a carrier of life, a life cup, a gift to the world.

Blood for blood.

Perhaps no one could ever repay the debt of blood that had been shed in that one winter of all the world's winters alone, but the thought of sustaining *one* life, instead of destroying one seemed to reverse a tide, to speak of creation instead of destruction.

I laid the magazine aside, lost in a new comprehension.

Gordon came back from the hospital, looking strangely happy for having just been relieved of a pint of blood.

"They think she might make it," he said. "She seems to be taking a turn for the better."

"Was Hong Sang there, did you see him?"

"I did," he said a little hoarsely and said no more.

When the decision came, it came gently, like spring in the village. There was no violent burst of color, no great revival from the dead, but only a gentle knowing, like a new warmth radiating from the earth or a different feeling in the wind. Yet for all its gentleness, it would have been as impossible to stop as the growth of a leaf or a seed, without killing something.

We looked at the apartment below the one Jean and Scott had signed for, and it was as simple as writing a name on a dotted line. We asked for two weeks extension on the village house to set our moving in order, and with a calm finality, the decision was made. Signed and legalized with a government stamp.

Then the backlash of feelings began.

At the Store, I ordered groceries in English instead of Chinese. Suddenly I could not think of the Chinese name for anything and found it did not matter. Hong Sang understood English.

"How's your little girl?" I asked between groceries being pulled off the shelf.

He turned around and faced me, looking directly at me, smiling kindly. The old hardness was gone from his face.

"She will live," he said quietly. "And I will never forget."

He paused, and I looked away, knowing that for both of us the stereotypes had been destroyed, that they had crumbled under the close contact of human existence.

He wiped his nose and tried to smile.

"I hear you're moving," he said.

"Right. In about a week."

"Never mind," he said soothingly. "You'll be happier among your own kind."

The words shocked me.

"Our own kind? Do you really believe there are kinds of people or that all people are equal?"

I saw him hesitate, caught between his ancient prejudices and his adult allegiances.

"Perhaps not different kinds of people," he conceded, "but there are people caught in different kinds of circumstances."

I bought the rest of the groceries and went down the stone steps, nodding to the shoe repairman and the sellers of seafood squatted along the road, knowing that what he said was true. There were people caught in different kinds of circumstances, caught in traps that the individual was almost powerless to overcome. In our time in the village we had consciously fought off the image of the change agent, the bringer of new things. Our role had been to learn, to absorb, to understand. But now that we were getting ready to leave, I began to wonder if we were not taking more than we had given, if we did not in some way owe something to the village. What had seemed like a proper sense of humility now began to wash over me like a sense of guilt.

What had we done for the village?

What difference had our being there made?

That evening Gordon and I discussed these questions and decided on a plan.

The old European who lived on the hillside had walked past our home, morning and evening, every day since we had lived there. Occasionally I would wave to him, or he would pause and nod his balding pink head, saying *goot effening* or *goot morning,* but that was all we knew of him. The boys had pointed out his house and the vacant house next to it, but beyond that he was a stranger to us.

But now that the news was loose in the village that we were leaving, he stopped by. It was one evening after his late swim. He was armed with a bouquet of wild flowers, picked along the grasses of the beach, and a huge smile.

"Flowers for you, Madame," he said politely. "I haff come to say how sorry I am you are mooffing."

We invited him in, put the kettle on for tea, and cut a piece of apple pie left over from supper.

"Ah," he said, eating the pie with relish, "if I had known there was pie in this house, I would haff brought the flowers zooner!"

I watched him eating and chatting, thinking what a shame it was that we had never known him. He was an interesting person, even if he was not Chinese.

"Where is your home, originally?" Gordon asked.

The old man laid down his fork and began to sip tea. There were faraway lights in his old eyes.

"Ahh. A long time ago, ofer thirty years ago, I left Sveden," he said. "I haff not been back there for many years."

"Do you have a family?"

"Oh yes, I haf a wife and some childrens who I haf not zeen for a long time. I . . . they came once with me to this place, to the East, long ago, but they did not share my enthusiasm for Eastern life. And so my wife, she left and went back to her hometown, and I stayed. I suppose at first we all thought that it was *temporary,* do you say? Yes, temporary. But zoon there was no life between us. They became more and more a part of the hometown, and I became more and more to loff this place. And now we haff become different peoples. I like my way of life, and they like theirs. We haff no time for each other. Look at me. I am a free man! How could I go back to all that entanglement of family? All those trying demands? Ahhk!"

He smiled and began to eat his pie.

"Don't you ever feel lonely or miss your family?" Gordon asked.

"Ahhk! They do well without me! And here I come and go freely. And even if I did miss them, it is. too late now. Too many years have passed, and I am like an old Chinese."

I watched him, thinking of the name the village children shouted after him. *The Fox,* they called him, and did not respect him as they respected their own elders. He had become lost between the sides, a nomad with no place to rest his heart.

And looking at him, I knew it was not a thing I wanted to happen to me.

"The house next to yours," Gordon said, to ease the tension, "is anyone planning to use it?"

"Not that I know of," he replied. "It has stood vacant for about five years. A man began to build it and ran out of money, and eventually the Kai Fong Community Council took it over. There was some talk of using it as a what-you-say a common building, a Community Center, but it neffer happened."

Gordon glanced at me, and I knew his plan was growing.

When Tommy came over the next evening, Gordon was ready to lay down a proposal.

"How would you feel about it if we opened up the house on the hillside as a community center," he began, "with a library, some game tables, maybe a snack bar, a place to play records, or hold dances. What would be the response to a thing like that?"

"Not here at your house?" Tommy asked slyly.

"No, No. We've been through all that. Anyhow, we're moving. This would be quite a different thing. We could get a crew of workers together to remodel it."

"Workers cost money. Where would the money come from?"

"I think I have friends who would be willing to contribute."

"And who would run it? You'd have to have someone there who would be responsible, or it would be torn apart in no time. We Chinese say that anything that belongs to everybody belongs to nobody."

"That's just what I was coming to," Gordon said slowly. "How would you like to be Community Program Director?"

Tommy looked at his hands.

"I have a job."

"If we paid you more?"

Tommy nodded his head. "It's a possibility," he said.

"Who owns the building now?"

"The Kai Fong."

"Do you think they'll let us use it?"

"You can ask," Tommy said.

The leader of the Kai Fong was considered the mayor of the village. His office was a shed where he carried on his kerosene business, filling drums and cans for the homes of the village.

They filed into his place, the leaders of the Kai Fong, serious, sober-faced men, aware of their responsibility to the present and the future. After a brief consultation, they came up with a verdict.

"We appreciate the way you have lived among us," said the leader, "the way you have learned, the way you have walked on our street. You have been remarkably free from the stupidities of your kind. But this last thing that you would do—we know that it is only because you are leaving us, and some of your old attitudes are coming back. There seems to be a strange feeling on the part of the foreigner that when he leaves a place, he must leave a monument to his name, a building or an institution he can point to and say, *that is the proof that I have been there.* But these monuments are sometimes a stone around our necks, they are too heavy for us. They introduce ideas that are not central to our way of life. They cost money that we cannot afford and usually set up one of us to carry out the foreign ideas, cutting him off from his own people and making a foreign puppet out of him. If we must speak plainly, let us say that we do not need these monuments to your name. While you were here, you have built a monument in our hearts that is much easier to bear. We believe that 'within the four seas, all men are brothers', and each man is responsible for his brother, but how that brotherhood is understood is a delicate matter."

All the old men sat in a straight row, staring at the floor, ashamed to have to speak such plain things aloud.

In the days that remained in the village, I walked the streets with a feeling of painful love, of looking back over the trail we had come, thinking with a tug of the moments of beauty, of the faces that lined the way. And there was still the feeling of a deep debt, of having taken an enormous, priceless treasure from this place.

Yet as I walked down the street by the wine factory and looked up at the sky leaking in irregular patterns through the odd shapes of the grey roofs, I understood. I could believe that somehow the village had changed by knowing us because we had been changed by knowing it. What had happened to one of us had happened to all of us.

And the idea of leaving something concrete to mark our passage left me forever.

I thought again of Tong's mountain, of the way we had come, slipping and sliding, learning and loving, and I hoped I could take the love of the village down the other side of the mountain, down the old-new path to *my own kind*. Exactly where that path led and how it twisted and turned, I was not sure. But I knew now that nothing was an end, that life would go on, imperceptibly changing from one state to another, like spring in Check Wan village.

transplanting
the papaya tree

I stood in the courtyard, looking at the brick wall and the friendship garden with a tightness in my throat. How cheated I had felt the day the boys filled the garden with flowers and plants, crowding out my coveted lettuce; Now there stood Tong's papaya tree, it's shaggy leaves growing up next to the wall, with roots deep in the soil.

How, for goodness sake, did one transplant a papaya tree?

To take all that root system along would necessitate a truck and to pull it up by the roots would kill it.

I went to the hardware store to buy a shovel.

I saw her, in the shadowy darkness of the street, her eyes big and frightened above a new pregnancy, the mother of the crippled child.

"Ding Tai," she smiled wanly, "I hear you're going to move house."

"Move house only, not heart," I assured her. "How have you been?"

"Ayie! Getting fatter every day!" she smiled, patting her protruding front. "Ah, Ding Tai."

"Yes?" I searched her soft, sad face, wondering what was coming.

"There is one favor I would like to ask, one thing to help quiet my heart."

"What can I do?" I asked almost too eagerly.

"I know there may be nothing that can ever be done for my child, but always I think perhaps you know someone, some very wise doctor who could help. Is there some such person that you could take a child like mine to see?"

I searched my mind. There was a clinic in the city where doctors and Sisters treated such cases, where some children were even kept in residence and given therapy.

"There is a place," I said, "I don't know what they could do, but we could talk to them and see."

Her eyes were begging, full of relief, sadness, and hope.

"Ah yah, if you would go with me, it would be good. You people have friends on the outside. The big doctors listen to you. How do I know they will help me if I go alone?"

"They're good Sisters," I assured her. "They help people all day long. This is their life. They wouldn't turn you away!"

"But I'm afraid. They may not speak Chinese. Would you go with me?"

"Of course," I promised, as much to set at peace my own feelings about leaving the village as to help her.

I went on to the hardware store, flooded with relief that she had asked.

My feet seemed to follow the shovel as I wandered back toward the house on the corner. I was propelled along, pulled ahead by the plants to be dug, yet the rough texture of the wine factory walls called out to me to stop and touch, and the weavings of the chicken crates called out to me to stop and feel. Beyond the beach, the boats did their mesmerizing dance, dipping and bobbing with the rise and fall of the waves.

Something in me wanted to throw the shovel away and stay in this painfully wonderful place, to throw my arms around it and hold it to me, to keep it forever, regardless of what it would mean.

Yet as I reached out to it, I knew the very fact of its impermanence made it priceless, appreciable, and tantalizingly desirable.

If I would clutch at it, possess it, and make sure that it lasted forever at any price, we might no longer hear the sea or be stirred by the textures or warmed by the smiles.

To come, to touch, to be touched, to go.

Responsive to, but not possessively responsible for.

There was something painfully creative in living like this, something close to the quick, *something not to be grasped at.*

I stood in the courtyard, stabbing at the dirt, wondering why I did not leave this job for Gordon. Somehow the friendship garden seemed the most valuable piece of furniture in the house. What else could not be replaced?

Ah Wai's soft slippers scraped across the cement behind me, and she coughed a small discreet cough.

"Missy?"

"Yes."

"What day are we moving?"

I looked at her, catching the "we."

"Ah Wai, sorry. Everything has happened so fast. I haven't asked you. Are you going with us?"

"Many people live in the village and work in Shallow Water Bay."

"It's not inconvenient? You wouldn't rather work for some foreigner over at the other beach?"

Her eyes were down.

"I don't speak English very well," she mumbled apologetically.

I suddenly realized that we had always spoken to each other in Chinese, so much so that I thought of her as being able to speak perfect English. I shook my head and did a retake.

"I'd be delighted if you want to come with us."

"Tisso. How could I leave Tisso?" she said. "The bus ride is short every day. What does it matter?"

I put out my hand, meaning to make it a deal, but the hand found itself on her shoulder, and the only deal that came out was one short name, spoken gently.

"Ah Oi!" I said.

And she did not correct me.

The call came before we moved, the appointment at the hospital for the crippled baby.

"We have time to see her Wednesday afternoon, if you can bring her in," said a woman's businesslike voice.

We boarded the bus on Wednesday afternoon and bumped our way to the downtown area where the hospital was located. I offered to hold the little girl part of the way, but she clung to her mother, who was already sitting uncomfortably on the hard bus seat. I watched the child, now over a year old, trying not to stare obviously, but observing. She was still tiny and frail, unable to sit alone, with a vacant look in her dark eyes; yet there was a pathetic sweetness about the child, a shadow of what might have been.

"How soon do you expect the next one?" I asked.

"About two more months," she said, and then as though she were reading my mind. "Maybe you wonder why I'm having another child when I did *this* to my third one. But how else can I go on living? Ah yah, somehow I have to try again, to prove to myself that it won't happen again, that I can erase the bad happenings with a good life. I have to prove it to myself and to my husband. He is a good man and said we would have no more children if I wished it, but I told him I must have at least one more."

She held the tiny, deformed child to her and kissed the top of her head.

The hospital was high on the top of a hill, with tall colonial ceilings, high windows, and whirling center fans. We waited for what seemed like hours before the nurse took a case history, and the doctor examined the baby. At last the sister in charge asked to talk to me.

"I'm sorry," she said kindly, "there's nothing we can do for this child. She's a sweet little thing, badly retarded, but will never be violent or cause any harm. Talk to your friend and encourage her to take the child home and include her in as normal a way as possible in the family circle. There is no hope that she will ever be normal. She may never talk or walk."

The Sister did not speak Chinese, and my friend did not speak English, and I became the bearer of the news.

I softened the words as much as I could, but how softly can you tell a woman there is no hope for her child? That there is no hope, even of death, but that it must live on and on in pain and shame?

As we bumped home in the bus, I thought of the tall, black visitor at the Easter Service and wanted to tell him that even my Caucasian face could not always work miracles.

Then it was moving day, and the sky hung in a grey fog over the sea, and the junks floated on the horizon like phantom boats from the beyond.

The moving lorry pulled up in front of the house on the corner with grunts and snorts and sat quietly in the swirl of the street while our belongings were carried from the house and stacked on the back. Curious onlookers lined up at the beach rail to see what had been in the house, and I winced to see our private lives stacked callously on the back of the lopsided truck. Wedged among the tables and chairs stood the papaya tree with the other plants, wrapped in its shrouded clump of dirt, ready for the perilous journey over the mountain.

The older children had gone to school as usual, and Jean had kindly offered to look after Chris. When the lorry was stacked with the main pieces of furniture, Gordon climbed into the cab and left with the drivers.

"You stay here and see that the last things come out of the cupboards and shelves," he called to me, "and I'll help them deliver these things to the new apartment."

I watched the truck lumber down the street, the fog from the sea penetrating the house and my spirits. There was an old raincoat left behind, and I wrapped it around me to stave off the gloom.

When they were gone, I roamed through the house, going from room to room. The furniture was gone. The curtains we had so carefully whitened were down and folded in a heap. The water was shut off; the telephone wires were disconnected. The refrigerator had gone on the truck. The stove stood in the center of the tiny kitchen floor, uprooted and powerless.

There were things to be done, and I tried to do them. I opened the door to the children's room and saw the greyness of the sea through the windows, the small heaps of toys still to be taken, a rubber sandal here and a sand pail there. I stared at them like a person slowly waking from a dream.

Somewhere I found the broom and tried to sweep a floor, but I seemed to be sweeping up thoughts and memories, and I was grateful when there was no dustpan so I could leave them in a heap in the middle of the floor, unresolved. Time kept passing, and somehow nothing was accomplished.

I reached in my pocket and realized there was only a fifty-cent piece there, just enough to take the bus. It was noon, and I was hungry and thirsty. I roamed around with my hands in the raincoat pockets, wondering what it would feel like to be in this state not as an oversight but as an inescapable way of life—disconnected, powerless, hungry, thirsty, caught in those circumstances it would be a little more difficult to understand the oneness of all life, to believe the lack of barriers. Perhaps this was how beggars felt or men who robbed and stabbed others on dark street corners. Perhaps the heroin addicts on the hillside felt like this and were deadening themselves to the pain.

Suddenly the house seemed haunted with all the ghosts of the dreams I had dreamed, as though everything I had believed to be true had died. I felt an overwhelming need to step outside.

Leaving the door ajar, I walked between the tall dark shapes of the wine factory buildings and down the street to the Chun's Noodle Shop. I only knew Chun Tai slightly, and that seemed better than going to someone I knew well at that moment.

The doorway was dark and narrow, and it was dark inside the room. The tables were pushed aside, and the Chun children sat in the middle of the floor, shelling shrimp.

Chun Tai looked up, surprised to see a tall damp-looking foreigner. I pulled out the lining of my pockets and grinned at her apologetically.

"Chun Tai, I can't face you for embarrassment," I said, "but would you have a cup of tea in your shop? Do you feed beggars?"

Her face was exactly like the face of the army of small shrimp peelers who seemed to live on our doorstep.

"Ah yah, Ding Tai, don't talk like that! Ahie-yah! Why didn't I come to see about you? Some neighbor I am, so busy making shrimp balls for tonight. Here, sit down. Drink this tea. Ah yah, Anna, go out to the restaurant and get some food for Ding Tai. So sorry, we don't have anything ready to eat here yet—"

"Please don't go to any trouble. Just a cup of tea will do!"

"Anna, go buy something for her!"

"What do you like?" Anna asked. She was one of Gordon's students.

"Anything you choose for me. I'll pay you later."

I sat warmed and humiliated, and vaguely grateful, sipping the tea and waiting, with visions of a delicious bowl of Won ton noodles or some fried crisp vegetables. But after half an hour when Anna finally came back with the lunch, it was a hard-fried egg sandwich on white bread and a cup of sugary, milky coffee from the restaurant up by the bus stop.

I took the sandwich and the coffee, half-laughing, half-crying, finally understanding that with the village people it was a matter of respect not to take my identity from me, even if I had been willing to give it away.

162

I stumbled back down the street with my hands in my pockets, encircled by the fog. The red NO ENTRY sign loomed out of the greyness, guarding the wine factory street with its painted warning. By itself I could have taken it, but after the fried egg sandwich, it was too much. Suddenly I knew I could not go back to the house on the corner. The door was unlocked, and the movers could come and take the rest of the furniture themselves or dump it all in the sea.

I resolutely turned and climbed the hill, and stood in the line that was boarding the bus for Shallow Water Bay.

The bus was crowded, and I stood hanging on to the iron railing, blinking and sniffing from the cigarette smoke of the man standing in front of me. The bus lurched forward, bumping and grinding its way through the town.

I stood hanging and swaying, a kind of stark sense of complete aloneness pounding through me.

This is the way it is, I thought with ironic detachment, *no matter how married you are or how many children you have, some of the most earthshattering moments in life come to you alone, in a crowded bus with some stranger's cigarette smoke in your eyes. That's just the way it is. Some rides you have to take alone.*

The stranger turned and looked at me, and I saw he was a man from the village and smiled. I did not know his name, but what did it matter? Perhaps there would not be strangers anymore. There seemed to be something vaguely familiar about everyone.

It began to rain as the bus ground up the mountain.

Gordon was cheerfully sweeping and cleaning out cupboards with Ah Wai when I arrived. On the back porch I saw the boxes of dishes I had sorted out of the kitchen in the village, hoping never to see them again.

"I thought you might like to rethink which of these you'd like to keep, now that we have more room," he said.

I looked through them, aghast at what I had decided to throw out. A wedding bowl, a gift from a friend.

Jean was watching the procedure from the upstairs apartment, offering to help.

"You've got it made," she laughed in an American way. "My husband hides under the couch until moving day is over!"

I laughed with her and wondered what it would be like to live with neighbors who basically knew all the same things I knew. What would we have to talk about?

We had moved so often that this fifteenth move seemed to happen almost mechanically. By dark the children's beds were up, the living room arranged, and the rest of the unplaced items stacked in our bedroom. Mike had his bunk bed set up in a cubbyhole that had once been the servants' quarters and was busy setting out all his private possessions. Ever since he had known of the move, he had spent his allowance for things from mainland China, and now his room was plastered with ancient Chinese gods and revolutionary Chinese posters. A red pot of fragrant sandalwood sticks smoldered on his table, and a Mao cap hung on his bedpost.

"How do you feel about it, now that we've moved, Mike?" Gordon asked.

"I'll miss the street with all that neat junk and all those people," he said, "but it's not that far, really. I can always get on the bus and go back when I feel like it. And I guess I'm glad to be here where the rest of the American kids are." He paused and looked at us. "How do you feel about it?" he asked.

That was perhaps more complex.

We pushed the boxes and furniture aside that night and felt our way to the bed, wearily grateful that the decision had been made. There was no turning back from here.

It was hard to sleep without the lulling sound of the sea. There was no rattling and pounding. The voices did not call their mellow exchanges, and no street dogs yelped. There was nothing but a strange and hollow quiet that finally resolved itself in exhausted sleep.

It was almost a week later that we sat on the front patio of the new apartment one evening. The yellow terrazzo of the front steps led into the green of real grass. Beyond were hedges and trees, and the smell of a charcoal fire. A stream ran under the bridge with a peaceful sound. It was suburbia, Shallow Water Bay, Hong Kong.

The patio was full of people, a kind of amalgamation of many parts of life. Tommy and the Jeng boys were assisting Gordon as he roasted meat on the rustic barbecue. The old European had come with a bouquet of wild flowers to warm the new house. China Pearl sat with Jean, talking spring fashions. Tong had come with a new girl friend and a painting to cheer our walls. One of Marita's classmates from the American School had joined our children, and they chased around the yard trying the slide and swing and the new basketball hoop nailed up on the garage. Christopher walked through the grass barefooted, looking curiously at the bottoms of his feet to see why they tickled. I realized that he had never walked on a lawn before that he could remember.

I watched the children, moving among the many different guests, taking the situation as completely normal. Perhaps they would never have the battle of barrier-breaking we had experienced. Perhaps they would have different needs, needs in reaction to ours, needs to build up walls for their own identity and security.

I looked up at the bamboo trees growing beside the house and the tall palm and the sturdy evergreen growing side by side in front of our door and felt a kind of consolation, a gladness, a joy, a freedom still sore from failing to be captured.

Tommy came from helping Gordon at the fire and sat down, smiling broadly and munching on a hot dog.

"Do they really make these out of dog meat?" he asked.

Now it was *my* culture that was being questioned.

"No!" I laughed.

"That wouldn't be so bad. Chinese sometimes eat dog meat. We say if its back is toward the sky, meaning it walks on all four feet, it can be eaten. What is in here?" he said, examining it curiously.

"I don't know," I admitted, "I'll have to look on the label."

"Why aren't you eating any?"

"I've had enough."

"How do you like your new house?"

I thought of his sleeping shelf in the crates behind the market stall and could not answer.

"Did you like the village better?" he asked quietly.

I did not know which way to shake my head, so I looked at him, mute and immobilized, not knowing whether it was because he still slept on a board or because I had been thrown again into so much material complexity that I wanted to cry.

"You should be happy," he said, patting my hand. "You're very lucky."

Tong came and sat on the steps. There was a girl with him, a pretty girl full of earthiness and candor. Her beautifully manicured nails were long and dug into the bronzed flesh of Tong's arm.

"This is my friend," he smiled, "I wanted her to come and meet you."

The girl seemed uneasy, and Tong explained.

"She can only stay a little while, then I put her on the bus to go to work."

"It's nice to meet you." I smiled. "Where do you work?"

After I asked, I wondered if I should have.

"In Wanchai, in a restaurant," she smiled, showing pearly white teeth.

They drifted off through the crowd, and the last I saw of her she was clinging to Tong's arm, making her way up the hill to the bus stop, balancing on high heels.

China Pearl cast a significant glance up the hill.

"She's a bar girl," she said not too kindly. "What Tong wants with someone like that kind, I can't see."

She went and sat beside Tommy, who blushed a deep red.

The crowd shifted and swirled, changing shape and form in the barbecue smoke. Soda tops popped and children laughed, and small groups of conversation formed. Scott had left for his first assignment in Vietnam, and Jean was waiting for word from him. Tommy had only a few weeks until his examination and was tense about passing. Wing's father was thinking about buying a family car, and he and the other boys discussed mechanics with vehemence. China Pearl was wondering how to get a job downtown without bringing Jeng Tai down into a fit of overmotherhood, and the old European was waiting, I knew, to see if there would be any apple pie.

Tong returned from the bus stop and joined the group.

"Your friend is pretty," I said.

Tong smiled.

"She likes me."

"Are you serious about her?"

"I think so."

"She . . . had to go to work?" I asked tentatively.

"Haih," he glanced at me, sensing my thoughts. "It doesn't matter to me what a girl is or has been, as long as she likes me. Some men, they say they only want to marry the good girls, the girls that never had another man. But that doesn't matter to me. One time I loved a good girl, and she thought she was too good for me. Now I am not such a good man myself . . . so why should I marry a good girl?"

"She says she'll marry you?"

"I think so. And when she marries me, then no other men. Only one. Me. No more working in the bar."

"Ayie, Tong!" Tommy interrupted. "How is she going to change her way of living? Is a marriage feast suddenly going to make her different? She is like a tigress. How do you know it will be only you?"

Tong's face clouded.

"I'll beat her to death if she looks at another man after she marries me," he said with sudden passion.

In my mind I saw the strong vivid colors of Tong's art and thought of chaotic personal lives, of the severed ear and leprosy-disfigured face of Van Gogh and Gauguin.

"Are you still working for the Englishman?" I asked, to change the subject.

Tong's eyes were flashing, showing an inner anger.

"I will never go back there in my life," he said bitterly. "I have sold three paintings now and have met other friends at his house who can help me. I'm going to find ways to live without his pig-dung money."

Under his smooth bronzed exterior, I could see Tong was trembling and I wished I had not asked him so much. He always looked strong, and it was easy to forget he was weak.

"I'm sorry if I upset you," I said, quietly, aside.

"Ayie," he sighed. "It is these things that cause the badness to get in my head. These questions are too big for me, like they will make me die. I like to be the free man and to have a free woman. It is all free until I love one woman, and then my head gets like the old ones, and I want to own the woman, even to beat her if I want to. Ayie, my head is new, and my heart is old."

And he covered his eyes like a man in pain.

But later, when we were all sitting on the steps eating the apple pie the old European had waited for so patiently, Tong seemed more relaxed. He closed his eyes, leaned against a pillar of the porch, and recited a Chinese poem, as though to calm his mind:

> San Kung, Suei juen,
> Ye mo lo.
> Lauh um, Fa ming,
> Yau yat chuen!

Tommy picked up the words and translated them for the English speakers:

> The mountain is desolate,
> The water is gone,
> And we have lost the road;
> Then through the shadows

> There breaks the brightness
> —There is a village ahead!

It was quiet for a moment. The shadows of evening had begun to creep across the grass, and the coals of the charcoal fire gleamed red under the palm tree. For a wavering second the wind brought the sound of the sea from far away, then it was gone.

Gordon broke the stillness.

"Why did the poet speak of a village?" he asked. "What is the story of the poem?"

"It's such a common saying to most of us that we seldom think of the parts or how it was written," Tommy said. "Each person takes the words and applies them to his own troubles. It's a kind of hope poem. But it does have a story behind it. A poor boy who came from a country village studied, worked hard, and became a high official, a judge, I think. As he observed the problems of the people who came into his court and the government's corruption in dealing with the poor, he had many ideas about how the country should be run. These ideas he wrote in the form of poems, and gave them to the rulers. But the men in power thought him nothing but a dreamer of ideas, so they did not take him seriously. He became very unhappy and filled with hopelessness. He felt that the world was so bad, it would end in his time.

"Then one day during a festival he returned to his old village and joined in the celebration with his family and old friends. When he saw them enjoying the festival, making their simple lives new with one another in the middle of green fields and wild flowers, he knew that hope had not been lost in the world, that from the lives of common people, goodness would come, and that it would be stronger than the corruption in high places."

"It is a hope poem," Wing said dreamily.

"But whose hope?" Tong asked almost fiercely. "Ayie, the world is hoping for so many different things now. In the East there is one set of hopes; in the West another. If everyone's hopes come true, what will be, can you tell me? It would still be all the confusion because what the people hope everywhere is different." He turned to Gordon, directing the question to him. "Ding Sang, what do you think? The way ahead, will it be the way of the West or the way of the East?"

Gordon was cautious, caught between his guests, wanting to betray neither side. "Perhaps the road ahead will be found by all of us," he said. "In the past, we have all come by different paths. Which of those paths can claim to be perfect? It could be that there is a point in the future toward which we all walk, and we will help each other find the way."

After the other guests had left, Tommy stayed behind. He seemed to need to talk. Gordon and I tucked the children in bed and sat with him in the living room on the floor. He picked up the guitar from the corner, twanging on its strings tunelessly.

"How's the test coming?" Gordon prompted.

Tommy looked up, his eyes large with worry.

"I'm very scared," he said. "And when I get very scared, I turn very Chinese, and all the English words run out of my head."

"Can't you take it again if you fail?"

"I could, but it would be such a loss of face. My mother wants me to get the good job, so I can bring home more money. All the boys need school fees, and it's hard for my mother to make so much."

Gordon hesitated. I saw him decide to bring up the question we had never dared to ask directly.

"Tommy, whatever happened to your father? Why did he leave the village?"

Tommy pinged a guitar string and looked at his hands.

"He lost all the money."

"How?"

"The Kai Fong controls all the gambling money in the village. One night my father got in a big gambling game and lost the restaurant. He asked for time to pay off his debt, but the old men of the Kai Fong said a debt was a debt, and they took the restaurant."

So that was Tommy's resentment toward the keepers of tradition. They had crushed him personally.

"And then they went into the vegetable business?"

"Yes, my mother and father, they started over again in the market, and when the new covered stalls were put in, my father saved up enough money to get a license and move into the good stalls where Lee Sang and Mok Tai work. He gave this money one day to Mr. Lew, the man with the bent back, and asked him to pick up the license downtown. You know Liu Sang?"

"Sure. He's the one who's always a little drunk."

"Haih, and he was a little drunk that day too. My father should *never* have asked him to pick up the license. When he went to the government office to have the license filled out, they asked him his name, and when he gave it, they filled out the license in *his* name. He paid the eighteen hundred dollars of my father's money and came away with a license for himself, old drunk Lew."

"What did your father say?"

"It wasn't important what my father said. What the town said was the terrible thing. They thought it was the funniest joke they had ever heard, and people could be heard laughing from one end of the village to the other. He gave old Lew eighteen hundred dollars to pick up a license, and Lew had it filled out for himself . . . ha, ha, haah. Everywhere my father went, people laughed in his face. Even the children on the street pointed to him and laughed. So in the night my mother packed up his clothes, and he went away from town. How can a man stand to be laughed at? When old Lew got sober and realized what he had done, he thought he was probably more clever drunk than sober, so he just got drunk some more and set up a stall next to Lee Sang."

"Couldn't your father take him to court?"

"What would be gained? By the time something is brought to court, the damage is already done. And how could he hire a lawyer when he didn't have five cents? No, sometimes I wanted more than anything else to get enough money to set up a stall next to old Lew, run him out of business, and let my father come back. But what good would it do? I can't correct the mistakes of my father. What he has done people will still remember and laugh behind their hands."

"So what do you plan to do?"

"Ah yah, I hope to pass this test, then I can get the better job at the bank and help my family."

"Does your father help the family at all?"

"Not very much. Somehow all the laughing at him killed his self-respect, and he no longer feels responsible. I feel very angry. Why should I take on his responsibilities because he has lost his pride? I do it for my mother, not for him. That's why I can't fail this test. How can my mother bear it if I fail her too?"

It was quiet, the night wind stirring through the palm tree outside.

"Would it help if you had a quiet place to study?" Gordon asked.

"Where?" Tommy gestured hopelessly. "The market is—"

"I know," Gordon said. "How about the room up over our garage? No one's using it. There's even a bed there, where the driver used to sleep. You could come here after work nights and study until the test is over."

"Of course!" I said, glad to relieve the feeling of deserting the village. "I'll include you in our dinners or save something for you if you're late."

We went out into the backyard to look at the room. It was a simple white-washed place with a small bed, a table and chair, and a few leftovers from the house.

"This would be good," Tommy agreed, thumping the mattress, "if I can make one change."

"What's that?" Gordon asked.

"If I can take that extra door leaning against the wall and lay it across the bed at night, so I won't get used to a soft bed."

"Don't you like soft beds?"

"Ah, that would not be the problem. The problem would be going back to sleep on the hard bed after the test."

The next morning I went across the bridge to mail letters at the post office, telling our families in America about the move. I glanced down the street at the row of apartment buildings. Beyond the post office was a bank, a beauty shop, and a supermarket. A block above us were the church and school, a filling station and a line of traffic. A *village* . . . I had never thought of this neighborhood as a village in the same sense that the fishing village was. It was more like an American neighborhood, with its stress on privacy and isolation, with none of the street living and openness. But if the discoveries we had made in the village were true, could they not make life richer here as well? The openness, the honesty, the willingness to care, the awareness of the need for interaction in other lives, the belief in the total presence of God wherever human life existed. Were these not portable values, ready to be lived out wherever there were people?

Perhaps if we kept the ideas alive, this community could be as exciting as any other village.

In my mind I understood it, but in my heart it was not yet resolved.

Yet even the Shallow Water Bay community neighborhood had changed greatly in the two years since we had left it, the year in New York and the year in the village. More of the residents were Asians now, and the distinctions seemed more economic, less racial. If Marita or Mike or DeDe came home with a friend named Evan or Mona or Lisa, the last names could just as easily be Wong as Smith, and they were children who spoke English fluently and lived in apartments that made our early corduroy look poor by comparison.

Marita came home one day from visiting in an Asian classmate's house, sighing over it's splendor.

"You should see Mona's house," she said enviously. "Those people have *class!*"

I tried to explain to her that class is not a thing built into the living room sofa, but she was too overawed to understand.

And Chris, delighted in the freedom of roaming a neighborhood where no dogs were loose and no trucks were allowed, sometimes forgot to come home. One day his three-year-old feet came pattering into the living room where I was sewing curtains for the still-bare windows.

"I think I'll go to Robbie's house to play," he announced.

I was glad he had a place to go but felt a bit of concern over paying so little attention to him since had moved. Our lives had flowed out. Had I neglected him?

"Why don't you stay home this time?" I suggested. "We miss you when you're always gone."

He cocked his head and looked at me.

"Would you say that again?" he asked.

I smiled at him, realizing he *had* felt the lack of mothering.

"I said, I miss you when you're gone too much."

"Say it again," he said playfully.

I picked him up and hugged him tightly.

"I really miss you when you're gone," I repeated.

He sighed blissfully and struggled out of my arms, then stood squarely on the floor with his feet wide apart and his hands in his pockets.

"Okay," he said, "I guess I'll go to Robbie's now."

"But I thought?"

"No, I'll tell you what, Mom. I'll go to Robbie's house, and you sit right here and *miss* me, Okay?"

I watched him go out the door, glad that one of us had his head together.

That evening Tommy went to his room to study. Jean came downstairs with her two children, and we sat on the front porch while all six children played on the swings and chased each other through the grass. There had been a telephone call from Saigon that Scott was fine, that several reporters had been captured, but that he was well and free. The phone call had sent assurance to Jean not to worry, and she sat on the edge of the porch not worrying, her pretty dark features composed in the patient smile of a woman who might hear momentarily that her husband would never return, while her children rolled in the grass. I sat beside her, feeling the silent communication of two people whose cultural roots have gone back into the same past and who can communicate without words, and I was grateful.

The darkness was coming, settling in through the tall palm and the lacy bamboo along the stream. Close to the porch, the sturdy evergreen grew as a silent token that people had been here who came from cooler climates, people who wanted to walk into the yard in the morning and be affirmed that the world they saw was the same one they had known elsewhere.

And there between the palm and the evergreen, in a sheltered spot against the stucco wall, stood the transplanted papaya tree. The village soil had been left around its roots and buried in a deep hole, *only four miles down the highway but centuries and light-years away*. And now it stood, looking limp and uncertain, a bit yellow around the edges in its painful new plot of soil.

I touched its leaves, wishing deeply to see it live.

the festival

Leaving an experience in a furniture truck, or wrapped in a raincoat crying on a bus, and worst of all, leaving it separately and alone somehow did not seem final. Both Gordon and I knew we had to go back to the village and leave it together to have some sense of peace.

One evening late in April, we left the children playing in the yard, and the two of us drove over the mountain to buy supplies in Check Wan market. For almost two weeks I had avoided going back, still feeling an edge of pain.

We drove into the market and parked under the familiar banyan tree, watching the stream of people go past. It was strange to realize that we did not live on this street anymore, that we could no longer indicate our house by a nod of the head from the market street. We were foreigners again, not again but yet . . . not yet but in a different sense. We knew these people, and they knew us; still they were themselves, and we were ourselves. We had come full cycle through the perilous journey of identification with others back to our own identity.

We opened the car doors and stepped into the street. The sound of pounding could be heard down by the sea where the opera house was being built for the Tin Hau Festival, and the smell of sandalwood was thick and rich under the branches of the old tree. I stood by the car, mesmerized by the rolling of the water and the dance of the boats, almost falling into the old fascination, but it was different.

"Did you want to get some things?" Gordon asked.

I nodded, not wanting to speak.

We went down the street past the Chun's carpenter shop, where the baby born when we came was beginning to walk. I had always meant to give her a gift and had never done it.

Wong Tai was sweeping up the day's shrimp shells, and Mok Tai had a fresh yellow flower hanging beside the red raw meat to be sold. I saw old drunk Lew and exchanged a look with Gordon, who shook his head. Lee Tai was weighing out greens on her handscale, waiting on her Western-housewife clientele, and up the stone steps by the Store, the shoemaker was closing shop for the day.

On Yau Tai's corner, she was sorting the day's baskets of greens while her eldest daughter cooked the rice over a street fire. The big smiling woman looked up and waved.

"Ding Tai, Ding Sang, Ah yah, where have you been? I wanted to come to your house and thank you for being good to my son. Ah yah, I'm tied to this market corner and can never get away, even to be polite."

"No need to be polite," Gordon said, in good Chinese form. "Has Tommy come home yet?"

"Haih. He was here a few minutes ago. Today he had his test. Ah yah, we won't know the results for several weeks. But let me give you some Choi Sum to cook for the children. Now don't tell Lee Sang. You tell him I'm not stealing his customers. He'd kill me! It's a gift for the children."

She laughed at her own joke, stuffing greens into a plastic bag and laying them in my hand. I looked clearly at the smile on her face and saw it not as simple joy but as a fierce grimace of survival, a determination to look life in the face and give it an earthy horselaugh. And knowing all that had happened, I stood on the corner in awe of this strong woman, this courageous person.

Around the corner and down the dusky street, the vendors fried and steamed their fragrant dishes, filling the air with an aroma that made me forget I had eaten. Down the left side of the street in the whatnot shop, the crippled baby's mother spooned gruel into the child's mouth. The woman's eyes were quiet now, sad pools of acceptance, and perhaps even hope, not for this one, but for the next.

Gordon reached in his pocket and took out a list.

"I have to go to the hardware store to get some bamboo poles and string for the kids at school to make banners," he said. "Do you want to go to the rice shop and get a few things there? It would save time."

I watched his lean, slightly bow-legged figure disappear down the street for a moment, then turned to go to the rice shop.

It was the same as the first day I had seen it, rough beams above the rice sacks, bottles of soy sauce and the vat of oil, canned sardines from China, and a profusion of cats and dogs. Jeng Tai was scooping out hot rice, and the fragrance overlaid the smell of burlap and sea water.

"Ding Tai! Come in! Have a bowl of rice!"

"Ah yah, sorry to disturb your meal. I'll come back later."

"Never mind, never mind; we always do business while we eat. Who can stop doing business to eat? Come in. Have a cup of tea."

I sat down and sipped the tea.

"Where's China Pearl?" I asked.

"She went to the business district for a job interview," said Jonathan, "and hasn't come back yet."

"Ayie, and it's late!" fretted Jeng Tai.

"She went with a friend, Mother. She'll be all right."

Jeng Sang sniffed his bowl of rice, silent and grim as ever.

"What kind of job can she get?" fussed Jeng Tai. "A factory job, making buttons, knitting sweaters. It would be better for her to work here at home."

"But ah-Ma, she *wants* to!"

I did not want to get drawn into a family argument and apologized for not stopping in to see them the day I left the village.

"We hear Chun Tai fed you a fried egg," Jonathan smiled. "Why didn't you come here? We would have given you a bowl of rice."

"Haih," Jeng Tai said reflectively, "Chun Tai doesn't know you." She paused and looked curiously at my face. "Wai, Ding Tai, there's something I've always wanted to ask you. May I ask you?"

"Of course."

"Was your mother Chinese? Are you half-Chinese?"

I looked at her, wanting to hug her, knowing that this was the deepest form of a compliment from Jeng Tai, the only way she could explain accepting me.

I looked down at the tea in my cup, smiling shakily.

"In my heart I am," I said.

It was terribly quiet over the bowls of rice.

The boys began nudging each other, uncomfortable with the emotion-laden air.

"And what's the other half?" Jonathan asked, to ease the tension.

"Half-devil!" I said, and we all laughed.

I left the rice shop with a warm heart and no rice, having forgotten to buy it, and walked down the wine factory street. Gordon had not told me where to meet him, and I found my steps taking me through the familiar old tunnel, where the smell of sour mash was so intense it made each breath a conscious effort. I glanced into the darkened doorway and waved to the ghost in passing. Strange, now the ghost seemed like an old friend with whom I had come to terms. I had gone from laughing at its existence to being terrified of it to meeting it face to face, and now the ghost in the wine factory was a symbol in my mind of the freedom I felt from fear—fear of losing approval or love or security. It was not that the need for love and approval was gone, but the *fear of losing* them was, and with it had gone the grasping use of these emotions to ensure security. Perhaps that was what had been lost—the desperate need for small securities; for in their place had come a sense of largeness, a quiet sureness of the all-pervading presence of God in life—God in me, which became a knowledge of my own strength and a kind of fearlessness. I was no longer afraid of life.

Down the end of the tunnel I emerged into the street in front of the house on the corner. I looked away, not yet ready to think of it. Past Chun's carpenter shop a shiny new car was easing its way through the profusion of children, dogs, and chickens. I looked at the driver, expecting him to be some posh Westerner come to take a stare at the quaintness of the village. Instead it was Wing behind the wheel, and Tommy sitting beside him.

Wing put on the brakes and pulled up, grinning broadly.

"Hey, show-off!" I called. "Now look who's sticking his teeth out! Where'd you get this thing?"

"It's my father's," he said. "I'm learning to drive. We're going to use it for the business and for a hire car."

I stepped back to admire the machine. I was no expert on foreign cars, but the neat circled insignia cut into a three-wedge pie caught me, wringing a kind of incredulous gasp from my mouth.

"Wha!" I said. "Why such an expensive one?"

"These cars are a good investment," Wing said matter-of-factly. "My father's business has been good, and what else can a man invest in here? This is a good car, low gas mileage, few repairs. Most of the taxicabs in Hong Kong are this kind of car, except that they use the diesel engines."

I listened to his sophisticated chatter, thinking of the day the Americans had come to the village dumping boxes of gift foods in front of Wong's stall. This Thanksgiving there would be a Mercedes-Benz parked in front when they came. Something about it made me laugh at myself, at everybody.

Tommy was not laughing. He sat on the other side of Wing, staring out the window distractedly, looking exhausted and discouraged.

"Tommy, how did you do?" I asked.

He got out of the car and came to where I was standing. He looked sick.

"I think I have failed," he said stiffly.

"How do you know? Your mother said you wouldn't know for a few weeks."

Wing started the car and drove around the corner.

"I was afraid, and all the words left my head," Tommy said, following the grey car with his eyes.

"What were you afraid of?"

His eyes were desperate, angry.

"I've tried very hard to learn your Western words, your Western ways," he said, "and if I could do it slowly and without pressure, *for fun,* like you have learned ours, I could enjoy it. But my learning of English is not *for fun.* It is a matter of the survival of my family. And when I knew that, when I realized what power other people have over me, and what results will come from the marks I make on a paper, it makes me angry. One time I told you I believe in myself, but now I know that is not enough. I do not have power over myself. The power of my life is in other people's hands. The people who have the money, the people who speak the right words and are born in the right families. I'm beginning to understand that I never had a chance, that it's too late for me . . . that I'm caught in a trap of being poor because I'm uneducated and uneducated because I'm poor. There's no way out."

I looked at him, seeing he had lost his little-Tommy-Tucker look, that he was no longer willing to sing for his supper, that he would take the plate from his keepers and throw it in their faces.

I followed his eyes along the beach and up the cliffs to where the buildings of the Farmer's Co-op perched perilously above the sea.

"Sometimes—if I fail—I think I will get some land," he said, "and grow things. Maybe we could manage to get a house up there."

"They wouldn't let your mother worship the old gods there," I said.

"The gods I can do without," he said, "but not food and shelter."

It was too much, the directness of his words.

"Tommy," I said, "I would give you my house and food, but what good would it do? Then I would have to move, and I would be poor, and what would be gained?"

He sighed and clasped my hand.

"Ding Tai, don't feel so bad about it. What can one person do? If you laid down in the street and died for the people of this village, like Yeso in your tradition, what good would it do? One person, two people, a handful can do nothing. It will take all the people; it will take laws and governments. Maybe, someday, my people in this place will live under their own words and in their own traditions."

I stood under the banyan tree where he dropped my hand, staring after him as he melted into the crowd and the street. Obviously, he could say no more. And I had no answer.

I went to the corner to wait, where the sound of the sea soothed the street noise to a muffled pattern. The evening procession of carts was passing, and I watched the women going by, pushing the sloshing carts in and out of the dark tunnel. After all the knowing and acceptance, how could I think of these women? How could we relate, how could we express the interrelatedness and yet respect each other's self?

I thought of myself, pushing a cart, living in a hut on the hillside, and I knew that I could—that if I had been born in the body of one of these women, I would have; then I remembered that the same life that lived in me lived in them, that they were the part of me with black eyes and black hair, doing this part of the world's work for me as I must do my part of the world's work for them, that each of us could be all things through the extension of his or her life into all people.

Across the street in the house I had loved, there were lights going on, and someone was pounding on the walls inside. I felt a stab of envy, a pang that someone else would live there, would possess the place that had been mine, would hear my sea, watch my boats, and listen to my wind in the banyan tree. And then I knew they would listen to them for me. They would be the part of me that lived in the house by the sea even after I was gone.

I leaned on the iron railing and looked out over the water. In the dusk the lights were going on in the sampans, one by one piercing the thickening greyness with pinpoints of light.

I breathed in the sea air, bent to touch the ground, and rubbed the sand between my fingers, understanding the fascination. These were the elements from which I came, the elements that would one day absorb me back into their fullness. It seemed simple to me now, the secret whispered by the wind in the banyan tree, known and long forgotten, half-remembered as in a dream. It was the stirring of God-the-life-force in all things, the interrelatedness, the oneness of all that was . . . the wind that blew up from the sea, that stirred in the branches of the old tree, that breathed in me . . . one.

And I stood in the wind with my feet in the sand, feeling whole.

There was a hand on my shoulder, and I looked up. Gordon stood beside me, with a bundle of long bamboo poles draped over his shoulder and a bag in his hand.

"I thought I'd find you here," he said.

I looked up at him, braced against the sky with the poles over his shoulder, his face full of a hundred things he could not say. There was an understated excitement about him, a look on his face I had never noticed. Suddenly I wanted to know him better, to know all the thousands of people he could be, now that I had come to know myself.

We were enveloped in the quietness, feeling the coming of night.

"I saw Wing," Gordon said. "He said he's seen you."

"That's some car he has. Did you see Tommy?"

"No. But Wing told me about Tong."

"What about him?"

"He went to the hospital about a week ago."

"Why?"

"He was afraid of the pressure building up in him, afraid he'd get violent and hurt someone."

I thought of beautiful Tong, and Tommy, and Wing, and I sighed.

"It's a crazy world. How can God love it? The dull followers of convention end up prosperous, while the questioners struggle, and the sensitive go insane."

"Did you think it would be any different here?" he asked.

The sound of hammering was carried on the wind from the flat green place at the base of the mountain by the sea.

"Do you want to go down and watch them building the opera house?" Gordon asked. "It's just a few days until the Tin-Hau Festival. They say it's going to be quite a celebration this year. The Kai Fong is going all out."

"I don't know," I said slowly. "For some reason I don't want to go down and look. I'm afraid I'll feel like a tourist; and besides, the more you resolve inside yourself, the less you need to be there, to stare."

He dumped the poles down on the sand, suddenly realizing he was getting a sore shoulder.

"Do you think we really did resolve some things by being here?" he asked, sitting down beside me.

"I should hope so. Maybe not the things we thought we'd resolve, though."

"Like participating in Third World living, teaching our children not to be prejudiced, and delving into our own integrity?" he asked, ticking them off on his fingers.

"Oh good Lord, was that why we thought we came here?" I asked.

"Then what did we learn?"

I sat running sand through my fingers. Above the street the tiled balcony of the house on the corner stood like a pinched and lonely crow's nest suspended over the crowd that milled beneath it. I remembered the morning I had stood there, looking over the street, breathing in the wind, hearing and seeing and feeling at a baffled distance, wondering what it all meant. And now, this evening, sitting on the street level, running the sand through my hand and leveling eye to eye with the crowd, I still wondered what it all meant; whatever it meant, I was now a part of. I was no longer the lady in the little white room coming out on the balcony to share my possessions, my tolerance, and my integrity because I had lost all these in the form I thought they had existed, and in their place had come a knowing so intangible the only way to express it was with a look or a touch.

I brushed the sand off my hands and touched Gordon's arm with one finger, looking into his face with gentleness and love.

"That's what I learned," I said.

I saw the warmth rise in his eyes.

"I wish I could kiss you," he whispered.

"Go ahead." I smiled. "We don't live here any more."

The crowd came and went, swirling in its kaleidoscopic patterns walking from village to mountain, pushing carts and carrying children, laughing, talking, taking home fish and vegetables tied in a string. I watched them, knowing why I no longer wanted to go down to the temple and observe the festival rituals. Here on this street corner was the real festival, the Festival of Life, the morning to night chant of voices communicating, faces smiling, tears and laughter, hopes and fears. Here on the street was where the festival of being was enacted, where the drums were each person's heart and the sacred foods were each family's daily rice. I had seen the rituals, the beating of the gongs, the special foods, and the burning of fragrances, but nowhere did the observance of life have such poignancy, such a depth as it had in moments of unconscious joy—of anger, of fear, of love and warmth, as the unknowing dancers acted out their own parts in the drama.

And yet the dancers, unaware of their own grace, always questioning the authenticity of their own movements, perhaps needed specified moments of consciousness, moments when they could observe their own being in ritualized form, where they could be assured that they were and would continue to be.

Gordon sat quietly, immersed in his own thoughts.

"What's in the bag?" I asked, picking it up.

He laughed and took it from me.

"A special present from two little old ladies," he said. "I stopped in the snake wine shop, and they gave me a bottle to try."

"They didn't!"

He held up a brown bottle with characters and reptiles on the label.

"Are you going to drink it?" I asked.

He winked at me and put it back in the bag.

"Later," he said.

I stared at him, catching a glimpse again of the multifaceted person I was just beginning to know. He had changed too, the man who used to shiver at the thought of walking over crabshells.

He stood up and held out his hand.

"Are you ready to go now?" he asked.

I took his hand and bounced to my feet, catching the double significance of his words.

"I'm ready," I said.

We ducked through the railing and Gordon loaded the poles for the joy banners on his shoulder.